NEW DIRECTIONS
FOR COMMUNITY
COLLEGES

Number 32 • 1980

NEW DIRECTIONS
FOR COMMUNITY
COLLEGES

A Quarterly Sourcebook
Arthur M. Cohen, Editor-in-Chief
Florence B. Brawer, Associate Editor
Sponsored by the ERIC Clearinghouse for Junior Colleges

Number 32, 1980

Questioning the
Community College Role

George B. Vaughan
Guest Editor

Jossey-Bass Inc., Publishers
San Francisco • Washington • London

EDUCATIONAL RESOURCES INFORMATION CENTER

ERIC Clearinghouse For Junior Colleges

UNIVERSITY OF CALIFORNIA, LOS ANGELES

QUESTIONING THE COMMUNITY COLLEGE ROLE
New Directions for Community Colleges
Volume VIII, Number 4, 1980
George B. Vaughan, Guest Editor

New Directions for Community Colleges (publication number USPS 121-710) is published quarterly by Jossey-Bass Inc., Publishers, in association with the ERIC Clearinghouse for Junior Colleges. Subscriptions are available at the regular rate for institutions, libraries, and agencies of $30 for one year. Individuals may subscribe at the special professional rate of $18 for one year. *New Directions* is numbered sequentially—please order extra copies by sequential number. The volume and issue numbers above are included for the convenience of libraries.

The material in this publication was prepared pursuant to a contract with the National Institute of Education, U.S. Department of Health, Education, and Welfare. Contractors undertaking such projects under government sponsorship are encouraged to express freely their judgment in professional and technical matters. Prior to publication, the manuscript was submitted to the U.C.L.A. Community College Leadership Program for critical review and determination of professional competence. This publication has met such standards. Points of view or opinions, however, do not necessarily represent the official view or opinions of the U.C.L.A. Community College Leadership Program or the National Institute of Education.

Correspondence:
Subscriptions, single-issue orders, change of address notices, undelivered copies, and other correspondence should be sent to *New Directions* Subscriptions, Jossey-Bass Inc., Publishers, 433 California Street, San Francisco, California 94104.

Editorial correspondence should be sent to the Editor-in-Chief, Arthur M. Cohen, at the ERIC Clearinghouse for Junior Colleges, University of California, Los Angeles, California 90024.

Library of Congress Catalogue Card Number LC 79-92023
International Standard Serial Number ISSN 0194-3081
International Standard Book Number ISBN 87589-810-6
Cover design by Willi Baum
Manufactured in the United States of America

This publication was prepared with funding from the National Institute of Education, U.S. Department of Health, Education, and Welfare under contract no. 400-78-0038. The opinions expressed in the report do not necessarily reflect the positions or policies of NIE or HEW.

Contents

Editor's Notes

Since Burton R. Clark published his *The Open Door College: A Case Study* and its companion article "The 'Cooling-Out' Function in Higher Education" in 1960, a small but constant stream of criticism of the community college has found its way into the literature. Unfortunately, community college leaders have often ignored the critics or, in some cases, have become defensive when criticisms of the community college have been put forth. It is hoped that the reader of this volume will consider the critic as one who expresses judgment on both the merits and the faults of the community college, and will view the questions raised here as positive statements on the role the community college can play and is playing. It is also hoped that this volume will be instrumental in offering suggestions for change.

The student and social protests of the 1960s brought to the fore questions of what higher education owes minority students, women, members of the lower socioeconomic groups, working adults, and society in general. It was during the 1960s that enrollments in the community college reached unprecedented (often unpredicted) levels. Community colleges promised much of what students and society were demanding: relevance, open admissions policy, special courses for ill-prepared minorities, low-cost education, night courses for homemakers and many other advantages. Yet during the sixties and even today, community colleges, according to some critics, have not fulfilled their promises and thus have failed to fulfill their potential.

In this volume, I provide an overview of the criticisms of the community college. Two of the authors, Burton Clark and Arthur Cohen, look back on their own works. Clark reevaluates his "Cooling-Out" article and Cohen does the same with his *Dateline '79*. William Neumann and David Riesman break new ground in their examination of what they call the community college elite. Richard Johnston proposes that community colleges join with other institutions to provide an alternate system of higher education. David Breneman and Susan Nelson examine the growing tension between the community college's broad mission and current funding patterns. Robert Templin and Ronald Shearon provide data which suggest that some tracking does take place in community colleges. Finally, Steven Zwerling questions whether the community college is at present adequately serving the part-time student.

I wish to thank Martha A. Turnage, vice president for development at George Mason University, for her encouragement and help in securing authors for the volume. I also appreciate the willingness of the authors to take time from their busy schedules to "question the community college."

George B. Vaughan
Guest Editor

George B. Vaughan is president of Piedmont Virginia Community College in Charlottesville.

Criticism of the community college has come primarily
from universities. The result has been a body of
literature that is detached, well researched,
and of value to the community college movement.

Critics of the Community College: An Overview

George B. Vaughan

The primary purposes of this chapter are to introduce the unfamiliar reader to some of the criticisms of the community college, to refresh the memories of those familiar with the criticisms discussed in the chapter, and to serve as an introduction to the rest of the volume. A secondary purpose is to present this writer's views on the role of criticism in the literature on the community college.

In introducing some of the criticisms of the community college, no attempt is made to conduct a review of the literature but only to highlight some areas of concern as expressed by a small but significant group of scholars. These scholars, with the exception of Steven Zwerling, view the community college from an external vantage point. As "outsiders," their writings have often been suspect by the supporters of the community college. Nevertheless, while there has been a dearth of criticisms of the community college, the ones discussed in this chapter have not only endured but continue to generate debate among educators. This volume will add new fuel to the debate. The results should be a better understanding of the increasingly complex role the community college plays in higher education and in society as a whole.

A brief discussion of some past writing by Burton Clark, Arthur Cohen, David Riesman, and Steven Zwerling provides historical perspective for the chapters these writers contributed to the current volume. Although Alexander Astin, Jerome Karabel, and Howard London are not contributors to the current volume, their writing is also briefly examined.

The community college in America has been relatively free from criticism. This is unusual considering the social and economic implications of a movement that promises postsecondary educational opportunities to virtually every American. Yet when one considers the following factors, perhaps it should not be surprising that criticism has been minimal: the rapid growth of the community college, much of which has taken place since World War II, and the grass roots support it has received; the relative newness of the community college, when viewed as a part of the total development of higher education in America; and the fact that the full impact of the community college (comprehensive programs, open-door admissions, proximity to citizens, and relatively inexpensive student costs) is simply not known. In spite of this rapid growth, newness, diversity, and limited knowledge of impact, some writers have made significant critical statements regarding the role of community colleges.

By agreeing to contribute to the current volume, Clark, Cohen, Riesman, and Zwerling (along with authors of other chapters) are acknowledging that the community college is a viable segment of higher education and one that continues to be a subject worthy of their scholarship. Moreover, some are acknowledging that their interpretations found in earlier writings are, like all interpretations, subject to review and perhaps change.

Before reviewing the writers' criticisms to be considered in this chapter, it might be helpful to introduce a general theme. In an earlier discussion Vaughan (1979a) pointed out that a major criticism centered around the contention that community colleges promote the economic and social status quo rather than aid upward mobility. Some critics claim this is done by the following means.

1. The United States has a hierarchial system of higher education with open-door community colleges at the bottom and selective four-year institutions at the top. Because of this stratification, the great majority of those who attend community colleges are doomed to remain near the bottom.

2. By offering inexpensive education within commuting distance, "blue collar" students have been encouraged to attend community colleges, thereby leaving the "prestigious" four-year colleges and universities to more affluent people.

3. Since community colleges primarily serve students from minority and lower socioeconomic groups, they function to limit these groups to low-status jobs requiring less than a bachelor's degree.

4. Community colleges have contributed to educational inflation and thereby have lessened the value of postsecondary education.

Some critics contend that members of lower socio-economic groups now need two years of education beyond high school just to stay even in society. There may be the false feeling of social mobility experienced by community college graduates, but their relative position in the social structure remains the same.

5. Community colleges *"cool out"* students by encouraging them to lower their aspirations from professional degrees to settling for career curriculum.

6. Cooling out often results in class-based tracking of students into terminal vocational programs that limit graduates to the world of the semiprofessional and technician. Thus, colleges serve as a "safety valve" to contain social and political pressure that otherwise might explode.

While not all of the criticisms discussed in this chapter or this volume fall neatly into the above categories, most of the critics of the community college ultimately have to deal with its social impact. Even Cohen, who devotes much of his writings to analyzing the internal working of the community college, alludes often to its role in the socializing process.

Critical Views

Clark (1960a, 1960b) was one of the earliest writers to offer a critical analysis of the community college. In *The Open Door College: A Case Study,* and in "The 'Cooling-Out' Function in Higher Education," Clark sets forth the thesis that community colleges enroll a large number of latent terminal students — students who aspire to transfer to a four-year college and receive the bachelor's degree but who are destined to conclude their education at the community college. "The latent terminal student is allowed into transfer curriculum but encounters counseling and testing that invite him to consider alternatives, subtle pressures to hedge his bet by taking courses that serve a terminal destiny, tough talk in orientation classes about realistic occupational choice, probationary status perhaps, and finally grades that will not allow transferring" (1960b, p. 163). In essence, the students are cooled-out by lowering their aspirations from obtaining transfer degrees to settling for terminal occupational-technical programs.

Since Clark analyzes the original concept of cooling out in his chapter in the current volume, it would be redundant to devote any great amount of time to his thesis in this introductory chapter. However, it should be noted that every writer discussed in this introductory chapter draws upon Clark's work. Therefore, anyone interested in the critics of the community college would do well to read Clark, for without an awareness of his writings it would be difficult to understand much of the literature. Indeed, community college leaders are indebted to Clark for bringing about a greater understanding of and appreciation for the role the community college plays in American higher education and in society in general.

In 1968, Jencks and Riesman published *The American Revolution* to almost universal acclaim as a major contribution to the literature on higher education. Today it is viewed as a classic in the field. Where did the community college fit into the academic revolution?

Jencks and Riesman classified community colleges, along with the general education movement, as the most visible part of a dissident movement which they placed under the title of "the antiuniversity colleges." In reference to the community colleges, and in words that rankled with many community college leaders, the authors noted that these colleges "recruit many of their faculty from the public schools and many others from former teachers colleges, hire relatively few Ph.D.s from major graduate schools, show comparatively little deference to professional academic opinion about how an institution of higher learning should be run, and consequently teach both subjects and students whom most scholars regard as worthless" (1968, p. 480). For many readers this statement conveyed the tone for the authors' discussion of the community college. (For contrasting views, see Morgan, 1979, and Vaughan, 1979c.)

Jencks and Riesman observed that many community colleges grew up with little sense of institutional purpose and with "hodgepodges of courses and curricula, established in response to real or imagined local demands" (p. 481). Nevertheless, the authors were quick to note that more and more people were devoting their professional careers to community colleges and that more and more students enrolled.

Following World War II, the belief became popular that virtually everyone should have the opportunity to pursue some form of postsecondary education. Jencks and Riesman saw this democratization of higher education as presenting something of a dilemma for society. However, they observed that "the community colleges provide a way out of this dilemma, allowing the universities to become more exclusive without the overall system's doing likewise. This, we would argue, is one major reason why they have won the support of both politicians and academicians" (p. 491). In essence, for the merit-based academic institutions of the 1950s and 1960s the community college served as a "safety valve releasing pressures that might otherwise disrupt the dominant system. It contains these pressures and allows the universities to go their own way without facing the full consequences of excluding the dull-witted or uninterested majority" (p. 492).

Jencks and Riesman ended their analysis by doubting that the community college would lead to significant innovations in higher education. They did not feel that community colleges could compete successfully with four-year colleges and universities for able students. Thus they concluded that "major assaults on the status quo [of higher education] will therefore have to come from elsewhere" (p. 492).

In looking back at some of his earlier writings, which presumably include *The Academic Revolution,* Riesman admits that some of his work on the community college was too general. In reference to Clark's and Karabel's writings on community colleges, he notes that there "has been an easy temptation to overaggregate community colleges as if they were all alike (a temptation from which the present writer in earlier work had not entirely freed himself)" (1978, p. 1).

While Riesman continues in a positive tone, he nevertheless sees the community colleges as less than perfect and, among other things, suggests that they "limit their aspirations in terms of their existing and potential strength, and thus . . . facilitate a division of labor among the missions pursued by both community college and four-year institutions on a statewide or, even more optimally, a regionwide basis" (p. 5). Riesman's final word in the article is a warning that community colleges should not compete with all other segments of postsecondary edcation — that they should not fall into the trap of "claiming to be everything anyone could ask" (p. 5).

Cohen is the most prolific of the critics of the community college. His best known work and his best volume to date is *Dateline '79: Heretical Concepts for the Community College* published in 1969. In this volume the author drew a picture of his vision of the ideal community college ten years into the future. But in order to reach this Camelot College, Cohen challenged many aspects of the community college of the 1960s.

Cohen was well aware when writing *Dateline '79* that to question the community college was "to call forth from its apologists the defenses erected over the decades when they were struggling to gain initial support" (1969, p. 51). But he did question on practically all fronts, from the college's mission to its architecture and campus location, from its programs of instruction to its instructors of programs.

Cohen challenged the community college for not defining its mission adequately. The community college, he felt, had not based its successes on outcomes but rather on processes. The college's identity was questioned from both inside and outside the institution. Moreover, Cohen felt that the community college had yet failed to demonstrate its effects. He declared that "failing students in courses and putting them on suspension *on the basis of undefined criteria* is accepted practice in the junior college . . . even though it is socially undesirable, pedagogically unnecessary, and philosophically immoral" (p. 74).

In discussing a number of myths associated with the community college, Cohen notes that the "cruelest myth of all is the one which perpetuates the fiction that junior colleges offer a liberal general education to their students" (p. 83). Cohen further challenged that the community college cannot "point to one instructional form which it alone evolved" (p. 87).

In a sense, Cohen (1971) picks up the critical theme of *Dateline '79* in *A Constant Variable: New Perspectives on the Community College*. The volume was written "because critical views of the community colleges are rarely seen" (p. xi). Cohen and his colleagues claim that community colleges sort and certify people and claim a mission that is less unique than community college leaders would have one believe. The author goes on to suggest that the "uncritical prevailing view that holds the institution to be a social panacea is shown to be unrealistic, short-sighted, and potentially debilitating" (p. 3). In this volume, Cohen criticizes institutional research (or the lack of it) in community colleges.

Cohen (1972) was highly critical of community services in the community college. He explained that the time when community services equaled instructional and student services was a long way in the future and in fact might represent an impossible dream on the part of community services administrators.

As Cohen moved towards his visionary "Dateline '79" his criticism of the community college continued. In 1976, he accused community college faculty members of "hiding behind the classroom door" and suggested that they "have become isolated within their own institutions" and that "the community college teacher has become a recluse" (Cohen, 1976, p. 24).

Cohen and Lombardi (1979) observed that the community colleges, during their growth and search-for-identity periods, saw an erosion of the university transfer function and that in fact "the transfer function was a marked casualty of the 1970s" (p. 25). Moreover, they propose that community colleges have moved away from the liberal arts toward remedial studies and indeed are not particular which students (including those who have bachelor's degrees) or which courses (such as "Tidepools in California") fall under the rubric of transfer.

Cohen does not ignore the social implications of the people's college. He asks if community colleges only want equality of educational opportunity or if they also want equality of results. "Continuing to offer only the opportunity to be rejected will surely court public wrath. The 'cooling out' function . . . is outmoded" (1969, p. 113). While Cohen points out that the community college has served as a safety valve to relieve the pressure on universities, he notes that a certain class stigma is attached to the community college, for "the fact that many students still pound at university doors demanding open admissions merely points out that some refuse to accept an implied second-class status" (1971, p. 182).

Cohen's many writings provide new and often exciting insights into the functioning of the community college. His work should be evaluated by anyone who is seriously examining the role of the community college.

Astin (1977), though not devoting a great deal of his total research efforts to community colleges, has nevertheless discussed them in enough detail to warrant a brief examination of his views. He states (1977) that while community colleges provide important services for adults, part-time students, and those pursuing technical courses, they may not serve students coming directly out of high school who want to transfer to a four-year college or university. He thinks the chances of students starting in a two-year college and later obtaining a bachelor's degree are less than had they started at a four-year institution. Thus Astin concludes that the community college does not represent an equal educational opportunity for the eighteen-year-old going directly from high school to college. He addresses the question of the "safety valve" theory whereby "educators in more prestigious institutions have probably supported community college growth because it represented a way of expanding educational opportunities that did not threaten their own selectivity and eliteness" (p. 248).

Astin feels that the change in behavior of students who attend community colleges is not as great as that found among students who attend four-year institutions. For example, there is less support for student power, a more traditional role for women, a lesser chance of assuming leadership roles, and in general less involvement in any number of areas traditionally associated with going to college. Part of the lack of student involvement results from the fact that most community colleges are commuter colleges and consequently are not able to compensate for the advantages associated with the residential experience.

Astin (1975) notes that minority students are more highly concentrated in community colleges and the least selective four-year institutions. In turn, the selective four-year universities with the least concentration of minorities spend three times as much per student as do the least selective two-year and four-year colleges (p. 6). This condition supports Astin's conclusion that gaining access to postsecondary education may not represent an equal opportunity. Many students have no choice but to attend the community college and thus are denied an equal educational opportunity.

While some of Astin's conclusions are sketchy and while much of his research has been concerned with the full-time community college student, he nevertheless raises questions that community college leaders and scholars interested in the community college should pursue in greater detail.

Karabel (1972) sets forth and discusses in detail a number of criticisms of the community college. Painting the community college with the broad brush strokes of one who has the advantage of viewing his subject from afar, Karabel seems able to relate to his own argument most of the issues raised by the social critics: "The thesis of this paper is that the community college, generally viewed as the leading edge of an open and egalitarian system of higher education, is in reality a prime contemporary expression of the dual historical patterns of class-based tracking and of educational inflation" (p. 526).

In supporting his thesis, Karabel discusses several concerns in varying degrees of detail: changes in the American economy which influenced the development of the community college, the community college as a safety valve, the community college as the bottom track of a class-based educational system, vocational education in the community college as the bottom rung of the bottom track of the higher education ladder, the failure of community college students to obtain the bachelor's degree, the cooling out of students, and tracking within the community college. In essence, Karabel has gathered many of the criticisms leveled against the community college and has built a strong argument that equality of education does not result from equality of opportunity to attend nonselective institutions; community colleges, rather than being the democratizers of higher education, are "in reality, a vital component of the class-based tracking system" (p. 555).

Karabel raises a number of questions, some of which are addressed by by other writers discussed in this chapter. He ventures rather deeply into motives when he accuses the American Association of Community and Junior Colleges, the Kellogg Foundation, the Carnegie Commission on Higher Education, Congress (through the Higher Education Act of 1972), the American Council on Education, and others of promoting vocational programs in community colleges in order that these programs be in their proper place while assuring that the needs of industry are met. Karabel sums up his argument regarding the vocationalization of the community college: "Paradoxically, the elite sector of the academic community, much of it liberal to radical, finds itself in a peculiar alliance with industry, foundations, government, and established higher education associations to vocationalize the community college" (p. 547).

Karabel's elitist stance and socialist solution often become hard to take for community college leaders who have devoted years of love and passion to the development of community colleges in America. Yet he raises a number of questions that, if not fully answered, should at least be considered and discussed if the social role of the community college is to be understood by its leaders, students, and society at large.

Zwerling (1976) is the only critic discussed in this chapter who viewed the community college from an inside vantage point. At the time of his major work, *Second Best: The Crisis of the Community College* Zwerling was a faculty member at Staten Island Community College. While Zwerling has moved on to New York University and while Staten Island has become a four-year college, his book remains an important contribution.

Zwerling's main thesis is his belief that community colleges have a hidden function in the educational process whereby they channel people into the same relative position in the social structure as that of their parents. He insists that community colleges maintain the existing social order rather than promote upward social mobility.

Zwerling challenges the more traditional histories of the two-year college in America. In discussing the founding fathers of the junior college, such as Henry P. Tappan, William W. Folwell, Alexis F. Lange, David Starr Jordan, and William Rainey Harper, Zwerling notes that "those theoretical fathers were not concerned with what came to be called junior colleges, quite the contrary; they were concerned about the university—the *real* university" (p. 43).

Zwerling maintains that, like high schools, junior colleges created a vocational track for students who threatened, if not diverted, to inundate the four-year colleges and universities. The vocational track was a way of providing large numbers of students with access to post-secondary education without disturbing the existing social order. Access to vocational programs was not an effort to democratize American society, but a move to the contrary.

Zwerling gives his own interpretation of the cooling-out function of community colleges. (See Chapter Two of this volume for Clark's discussion of Zwerling's views on cooling out.) Zwerling devotes a chapter of his book to heating up, whereby cooling out is replaced by a process that results when community colleges become student centered.

Playing the role of supercritic, Zwerling provides his classification of the critics of the community college. He divides them into four groups: the official critics, the left-official critics, the antiuniversity critics, and the radical critics. The Zwerling book, while leaving some loose ends and offering few workable solutions to the problems is nevertheless worthwhile reading for the serious student of the community college.

London (1978) is a relative newcomer to the ranks of critics of the community college. He conducts a "field investigation of the culture of one community college and how that culture is related to the larger social system in which it exists" (p. xii). He feels that the urban comprehensive community college that serves predominantly white working class students is representative of the type that is growing most rapidly.

The purpose of his study was to uncover basic knowledge of a community college's culture. (For a contrary view, see Vaughan, 1979b.)

London, like others among the critics, asserts that the community college he studied (which he calls City Community Colleges — CCC) serves to reinforce the student's social class and magnifies the frustrations of the world of the blue-collar home and the "blue-collar student." The students at CCC are filled with self-doubts linked strongly to their social class. CCC's proletariat students fear success while struggling to avoid failure. They are struggling against the middle-class values of their teachers and against the role society has carved for them — a role London feels CCC is dedicated to preserving.

London later traces the career paths of CCC's faculty and relates those paths to the faculty members' identities and perspectives. London concludes that many of the faculty members at CCC view themselves as less than successful; moreover, once they admit to themselves that they are not going to get the Ph.D., they realize that they are never going to teach in a four-year college or university. Career goals have to be changed. By redefining their career aspirations, the faculty at CCC "cushion themselves against the precariousness, strains, and tensions of their careers" (p. 40). As Clark points out in Chapter Two, London views the faculty members as being cooled out.

In reading the London volume, one should be aware that the college he studied was in its first year of operation, served primarily white students from blue-collar families, and was located in Boston — attributes which are not typical of most community colleges today. Thus London's claim that the college he studied is representative of a kind of community college that is growing faster than any other should be viewed with caution. In fact, anyone who has ever worked in a commuity college during its first year of operation must view the London study as taking place at perhaps the most atypical time in the college's history.

London fails to link CCC to the broader scheme of higher education and makes no major attempt to link it with the highly diverse field of community college education. While his study is narrow, it is useful for those interested in a highly critical work on a single community college. London gives us some ideas of how some students and some faculty members feel about one community college.

Value of Criticism

The foregoing discussion raises the question: Should community college leaders be concerned with criticisms which are, for the most part, raised by an extremely small group of university-based scholars? If the answer is yes, the next question might be why? One answer is that the critics offer new ways of looking at old problems and new ideas for exploration. For example, one can only estimate how many colleges turned to measurable instructional objectives after the publication of *Dateline '79.*

While this writer strongly believes that more writings of a critical nature should be done by community college faculty members and administrators, there appear to be certain advantages associated with viewing a movement from the vantage point of the university. The university professor is unlikely to be caught up in the day-to-day operation of the community college and is therefore unlikely to become as emotionally involved.

While detachment does not guarantee objectivity, it is nevertheless easier to be objective when one does not have a vested interest in the success or failure of an institution. And while being university based does not guarantee good research, it does mean that more emphasis is placed on research than is normally found in a community college.

How, if at all, can community college leaders profit from criticisms of their institutions? The following observations might be useful in answering this question.

Community college leaders should examine the criticisms and determine which ones are valid in a given situation. All of the criticisms discussed in this chapter and in this volume have validity for some community colleges at some point in their development.

If community colleges are at the bottom of the higher education hierarchy as some critics claim, does this mean that they are not fulfilling their mission? One could argue that if community college student bodies were not made up of a large percentage of members from lower socioeconomic groups, minorities, and others who have historically been outside the mainstream of higher education, the colleges would not be doing what they were designed to do. Probably a more valid criticism is that community colleges are not concerned *enough* with serving those individuals previously excluded from higher education and that greater effort should be exerted to serve them, no matter where the critics place community colleges in the higher education hierarchy.

In relation to the above, it might well be that the future will see a tilting of the educational pyramid which could result in many two-year programs moving up the hierarchy. For example, as more and more liberal arts majors fail to find suitable employment and as the economy demands more graduates from technical programs, the pyramid may shift. If it does so significantly, the fact that the critics dealt with the higher education hierarchy in the first place will provide a sociological and historical perspective from which to view the changing role of the community college in relation to the rest of higher education.

One of the most difficult of the criticisms relates to whether equal access to higher education represents equal educational opportunity. Perhaps the key is to be found in defining what is meant by educational opportunity. Few would argue that the first-generation college student from a lower socioeconomic group would have the same opportunity to move into the business or professional world at the same level as would the Caucasian offspring of a fourth-generation ivy league family. On the other hand, the opportunity to attend a community college might well represent an equal educational opportunity based on relative standing for those groups who in the past had no opportunity for education beyond high school. That is, short of a radical restructuring of society as suggested by some critics, the movement up the socioeconomic scale will continue to be intergenerational for most groups of people. Upward mobility in America has historically been evolutionary rather than revolutionary. A key to the evolutionary process is the nation's educational system. Today, community colleges serve as a major stepping-stone in the educational hierarchy for many members of the lower socioeconomic groups and thus, relatively speaking, do provide an equal educational opportunity.

In relation to the above, community colleges should be sensitive to the charge that they track students into vocational programs. How many individual colleges follow lower socioeconomic students to see if they do indeed end up in a vocational track? If tracking takes place, community colleges should examine how these students are being counseled, what role developmental programs might play to encourage them to enter the higher-level technologies and transfer programs, and in general assure that equal opportunity is available to all students within a given college. Tracking students tends to pervert the evolutionary process discussed above and does indeed represent an unequal educational opportunity for those students who are channeled into dead-end programs.

Cooling out might well be viewed in relative terms. Is one providing good counseling or is one promoting class-based tracking to advise a student to enroll in a program in which he can succeed rather than pursue a goal that is likely to lead to failure? Community college leaders could profit from a closer examinations of Clark's definition of cooling out and determine what the legitimate role of the community college might be in relation to it. It might well be determined that cooling out students is a legitimate role for community colleges.

As discussed in this chapter, several of the critics allude to the safety valve function of the community college. The safety valve thesis is dead or dying as the number of high school graduates declines. Assuming the thesis were valid, what roles were forced on the community colleges as a result of plugging the holes in the higher education dam to keep it from bursting? If the critics were correct in viewing community colleges as safety valves, are the colleges now ready to redefine their mission based on a lack of eighteen-to-twenty-one year old students? As the student recruitment wars reach new and more vicious levels, will community colleges be relegated to the status of vocational schools with a sprinkling of developmental and "community services" courses? Without critically examining these questions and tailoring programs based upon the findings, the community college is likely to go off in all directions in search of a new identity. Simply using terms such as lifelong learning and community-based education will not substitute for a critical examination of the role community colleges are to play in the future.

Finally, community colleges are important enough to higher education not only to examine what the critics are saying but also to encourage critical views from both inside and outside the field of community college education.

Much can be learned from the critics. Simply to ignore what they say or, worse yet, to become defensive when criticized is to ignore the value of critical analysis. Ironically, many community college leaders were trained in disciplines which emphasized the vital role of the critic, yet when it comes to the community college movement and especially to the role a single college plays in that movement, a certain paranoia seems to emanate from community college leaders. Paranoia is a form of mental illness; critical analysis is essential to mental health. Community college leaders have a choice between the two approaches. This writer and this volume make a plea for critical analysis. The result will be a healthier approach to defining the role of the community college of the future.

References

Astin, A. W. *Four Critical Years: Effects of College on Beliefs, Attitudes, and Knowledge.* San Francisco: Jossey-Bass, 1977.

Astin, A. W. *The Myth of Equal Access in Public Higher Education.* Paper presented at the Conference on Equality of Access in Post-secondary Education (Atlanta, Georgia, July, 1975). 32 pp. (ED 119 551).

Clark, B. R. "The 'Cooling-out' Function in Higher Education." *The American Journal of Sociology,* 1960, *65* (6), 569–576.

Clark, B. R. *The Open Door College: A Case Study.* New York: McGraw-Hill, 1960b.

Cohen, A. M. *Dateline '79: Heretical Concepts for the Community College.* Beverly Hills: Glencoe Press, 1969.

Cohen, A. M. and others. *A Constant Variable: New Perspectives on the Community College.* San Francisco: Jossey-Bass, 1971.

Cohen, A. M. "Hiding Behind the Classroom Door." *The Chronicle of Higher Education,* 1976, *12* (20), 24.

Cohen, A. M. "The Twilight Future of a Function." *Community Services Catalyst,* 1972, *3* (2), 7–16.

14

Cohen, A. M., and Lombardi, J. "Can the Community Colleges Survive Success?" *Change,* 1979, *11* (8), 24–27.

Jencks, C., and Riesman, D. *The Academic Revolution.* New York: Doubleday, 1968.

Karabel, J. "Community Colleges and Social Stratification." *Harvard Educational Review,* 1972, *42* (4), 521–562.

London, H. B. *The Culture of a Community College.* New York: Praeger, 1978.

Morgan, D. A. "Beyond Contempt: The University Mentality and the Community College." *The Community Services Catalyst,* 1979, *9* (3), 6–10.

Riesman, D. "Community Colleges: Some Tentative Hypotheses." *The Community Services Catalyst,* 1978, *8* (2), 1–5.

Vaughan, G. B. "The Challenge of Criticism." *Community and Junior College Journal,* 1979a, *50* (2), 8–11.

Vaughan, G. B. "A Review of H. B. London's *The Culture of a Community College." Community/Junior College Research Quarterly,* 1979b, *4* (1), 81–83.

Vaughan, G. B. "University Mentality or Community College Paranoia: A Critique of Don Morgan's Reaction to David Riesman's Tentative Hypothesis." *The Community Services Catalyst,* 1979c, *9* (3), 11–13.

Zwerling, L. S. *Second Best: The Crisis of the Community College.* New York: McGraw-Hill, 1976.

George B. Vaughan is president of Piedmont Virginia Community College in Charlottesville.

The cooling out function — like democracy — is not very attractive until you consider its alternatives. It is likely to remain an important part of what American community colleges do.

The "Cooling Out" Function Revisited

Burton R. Clark

In the mid 1950s, after finishing a dissertation on the character of adult schools (Clark, 1956), I became interested in doing a similar analysis of community colleges. While teaching at Stanford, I spent a summer visiting a number of colleges in the San Francisco Bay Area to explore the feasibility of such research, particularly to weigh the advantages and disadvantages of a case study rather than a comparative analysis of several colleges. I decided to take my chances by concentrating on the college and getting to know it well, looking for connections among the parts of the organization in order to characterize it as a whole. The college I selected was a relatively new one in San Jose that offered entrée and was within easy commuting of Palo Alto. The fieldwork of the study and manuscript preparation during a period of three years or so led to a book and an article published at the end of the decade (Clark, 1960a, 1960b). The book covered the emergence and development of the college. It attended to unique features, but emphasized characteristics that, on the basis of available comparative data, a few side glances, and some reasoning, seemed to be shared with most other public two-year institutions and hence could be generalized — something to lay on the table that could be checked by others elsewhere and might, in explanatory power, be worth their time and effort. I spoke of the character of the community college in such terms as diffuse commitment and dependency on an unselected external social base; pointed to roles it played in the larger educational structure in acting as a screening agent for other colleges at the same time that it opened wider the door to higher education; and suggested that such colleges have particularly sharp problems of identity, status, and autonomy.

Foremost among the generalizations was the "cooling-out" function, a conception that clearly has also been seen by others as the most important conclusion of the study. My purpose in this chapter is to review the concept twenty years later. In retrospect, was it appropriate in 1960? Does it still pertain? How has it been used by others? Since its crucial features are often overlooked, I begin by reviewing the original idea. I then explore the possible alternatives to this particular function as a way of understanding the reasons for its existence. In light of the experiences of our own and other countries during the last two decades, we can better understand the alternatives now than we could twenty years ago. Finally I take up some ways that the idea has been used by others and conclude with a judgment on the value of the concept.

Original Conception

At the outset of the research, cooling out was not on my mind, either as a phenomenon or as a term. As I proceeded in my observations, interviews, and readings of available documents and data, I was struck with the discrepancy between formal statements of purpose and everyday reality. A poignant part of reality was the clear fact that most students who were in the transfer track did not go on to four-year colleges and universities. What happened to them? It turned out that the college was concerned about them, both as individuals and, in the aggregate, as a persistent administrative problem that would not go away. Emerging procedures could be observed that were designed to channel many such students out of transfer programs and into curricula that terminated in the community college. As I observed teachers and students, and especially counselors who seemed central to what was going on, it became clear that such reassignment of students was not easy.

It involved actions that, no matter how helpful, would be felt by many involved to be the dirty work of the organization. This effort to rechannel students could have been called "the counseling process" or "the redirection-of-aspirations process" or "the alternative-career process" or by some other similarly ambiguous term so heavily used in education and sociology. I played with the terms then readily available but all seemed to have the analytical bite of warmed-over potatoes. While I was stewing about how to point a concept, a friend called my attention to an article by Goffman (1952) in which, for various sectors of society, the need to let down the hopes of people was analyzed brilliantly. Goffman used terms from the confidence game in which the aspirations of the "mark" to get rich quick are out-of-line with the reality of what is happening to him or her, and someone on the confidence team is assigned the duty of helping the victim face the harsh reality without blowing his mind or calling the police. Now there was a concept with a cutting edge! So I adopted and adapted it, aware that it would not make many friends in community college administrative circles.

How did cooling out appear to happen in educational settings? Moore has summarized well the argument that I originally put forth.

> The process as described by Clark entails a student's following a structured sequence of guidance efforts involving mandatory courses in career planning and self-evaluation, which results in "reorientation" of the student rather than dismissal. The process begins with preentrance testing, which identifies low-achieving students and assigns them to remedial classes. The process is completed when the "overaspiring student" is rechanneled out of a transfer program and into a terminal curriculum. Throughout the process the student is kept in contact with guidance personnel, who keep careful track of the student's "progress."
>
> The generalizable qualities of cooling out as Clark saw them involve *offering substitutes or alternatives* to the desired goal (here a transfer program); *encouraging gradual disengagement* by having the student try out other courses of study; *amassing objective data* against the preference in terms of grades, aptitude tests, and interest tests; *consoling and counseling* the student through personal though "objective" contacts; and *stressing the relative values of many kinds* of persons and many kinds of talents other than the preferred choice (Moore, 1975, pp. 578–579).

Crucial components of the process that were stressed in the original statement and that I would want to emphasize even more now are that (1) alternatives are provided—the person who is to be denied a desired goal is offered a substitute; and (2) aspiration is reduced in a "soft" consoling way, easing the pain and frustration of not being able to achieve one's first goal and the difficulties involved in switching to and learning to value the offered alternative education and career.

Once I had virtually "seen" the process in operation in one community college it was easy to generalize. After all, the community colleges in general embraced the open-door philosophy and hence were unselective on the input side, while necessarily facing the standards of four-year colleges and universities and being somewhat selective on the transfer/output side. Figures were readily available for all community

colleges in California and the nation as a whole that showed how many students entered the transfer track and how many came out of it. And, there was no evidence that community colleges anywhere in the country took the traditional stern approach that students who could not for one reason or another do the transfer work were failures who should be sent away. To the contrary, the attitude expressed everywhere was a generous and open one that the community college should not label students as failures; instead students should be helped as much as possible "to find themselves" and to find courses and career objectives appropriate to their abilities.

Hence a general assertion was warranted: its specific steps might vary, and colleges might or might not be effective in carrying it out, but the cooling out process would be insistently operative in the vast majority of American public two-year colleges. This was necessary given the position of the two-year units in the general educational structure and the institutional roles that had emerged around that position.

Alternatives

One way to enlarge our understanding of this phenomenon is to place it in the context of alternatives. Can it be subordinated or replaced by other ways of proceeding? How could the roles of community colleges be so altered that the process would be unnecessary? Indeed, what has been done at other times and is presently done in other places that reduces greatly the play of this process? Six alternatives come to mind, a set that comes close to exhausting the broad possibilities. As backdrop for these alternatives, let us keep in mind that the cooling out process in community colleges is rooted in (1) open door admissions, a policy of nonselection; (2) the maintenance of transfer standards, an attitude that those who transfer should be able to do course work in four-year colleges and universities; and (3) the probable need to deny some aspirants the transfer possibility and to face the problem of what to do with them.

Preselection. One clear alternative is preselection, either in earlier schooling or at the doors of the colleges. National systems of education continue to select students at the secondary level, indeed to have specialized schools that are terminal. This form of selection remains the model pattern in Europe and around the world, despite the efforts to "democratize" and universalize secondary education in so many countries in the last two decades. The secondary school graduates who qualified for higher education, in the most generous estimates, were still no higher in the early and mid 1970s than 30 percent of the age group in West Germany, 35 percent in Italy, and 45 percent in France (Furth, 1978). Of course, in the United States, automatic or social promotion of students during the secondary schooling has been the opposite of selection, amounting to mass sponsorship. Some selection still takes place, particularly through assignments to curricular tracks within the comprehensive school, but it is minor compared to the dominant international mode. Current efforts to stiffen standards of secondary school graduation in the United States will, if effective, tend to increase preselection.

Naturally, selection can also take place at the doors of community colleges, no matter what the extent of selection at the secondary level. Some minor amount of selection perhaps takes place in some community colleges in certain regions, particularly in the Northeast where the long dominance of private higher education has left a legacy of selection for quality and low regard for the more open-door public institutions.

The greater the selection in the secondary school or at the doors of the colleges, the less the need to select within the doors. The gap between aspirations and scholastic ability is narrowed, since a higher threshold of ability is established. Every increase in selectivity reduces the conditions that generate the cooling out process.

This alternative runs against the grain of American populist interpretations of educational justice which equate equity with open doors. The reestablishing of sharp secondary school selection or the closing of the open door is not what most critics and reformers have in mind. But we need to keep preselection in view if we want to understand why most countries in the world currently have considerably less need for a cooling out function than the American system of the last quarter-century and the foreseeable future. The traditional injunction is a simple one: If you want to reduce cooling out, keep out the candidates for cooling out.

Transfer-Track Selection. All right, community college personnel can say, we have an open door but we certainly do not have to let every Tom, Dick, and Harry—and their female counterparts—declare him- or herself to be a four-year college student and set sail in the courses that give credit for later transferring. We will stop the "nonsense" of everyone having a chance and, instead, openly select at the doors to the transfer program. Those who appear likely to be latent terminals, if we do not select, will now be manifest terminals from the outset, and hence the need for the cooling out process will be drastically reduced.

This alternative is logical enough, certainly to the academic mind or the conservative critic, and it surely occurs to a minor degree in many community colleges. A quick and honest no at the outset, proponents would say, is better for the student, the faculty, and the institution than a drawn-out, ambiguous, and manipulative denial in the style of cooling out. But, logical or not, this alternative is also not likely to carry the day in American reform. The open-door philosophy is too ingrained; community colleges evermore define their boundaries loosely; almost anyone, part- or full-time, can enroll in courses offering transfer credit; and, besides, students are now in short supply and colleges generally for the foreseeable future will be less rather than more particular.

Open Failure. Perhaps the basic alternative to cooling out is unequivocal dismissal or withdrawal. This response is a classic one, found in the United States in the recent past in the state universities that felt it was politically necessary to have virtually open-door admission but then proceeded to allow the faculty to protect standards and slim the flow of students by weeding out in the first year those "who cannot do the work." Processes of admit-and-dismiss are widely operative in other countries, particularly where the forces pressing for more access are able to block sharp selection at the doors of the system but, at the same time, faculties remain free to flunk or discourage to the point of self-dismissal as many students as they wish in the first year or two.

As pointed out in my original formulation, this alternative is a hard response in the sense that failure is clearly defined as such: it is public, with the student required to remove himself from the premises. It is a rather harsh form of delayed denial—"we have to let them in but we do not have to keep them"—and can be viewed from inside or outside the system as heartless, a slaughter of the innocent. One role of the community college, as the most open segment in the American differentiated system, has been to lessen the need for this response in the state universities and public four-year colleges. The academically marginal and less promising students have been protected from the open-failure form of response by removing them from the settings where it was most likely to occur. Cooling out has been the "softer" response of never dismissing a student but instead providing him or her with an alternative.

This open-failure alternative is also one not likely to carry the day in the United States. Those who are most critical of community colleges do not seem to have it in mind and nowhere does it appear on the agenda of reform. Old-fashioned toughness—"You have failed, so get out of here!"—is not about to be reestablished as a general mode, either in two-year or most four-year colleges.

Guaranteed Graduation. In this alternative we take the social or automatic promotion of students that has characterized much of American secondary education in recent decades and apply it to post-secondary education. As an ideal type, the formulation reads: Let everyone in who wishes to come and let all who persist graduate. In the transfer part of the two-year college, this means let all complete the two years of work, receive the associate in arts or associate in science degree, and transfer to whatever four-year colleges will accept them. Standards are then not directly a problem since students will be allowed to graduate and transfer without regard to scholastic achievement or academic merit. The cooling out effort is no longer required.

This alternative is attractive for many participants and observers, especially those for whom equality is the primary value in higher education to the point of moving beyond equality of access and opportunity to equality of results. It surely is operative to some degree in numerous unselective four-year as well as two-year colleges: once the student is in, the college has a strong interest in seeing that he or she receives a degree. However, this alternative does not serve competence very well and debases the value of degrees, threatening the credibility and legitimacy of postsecondary institutions. It contributes to the inflation of educational credentials whereby individuals must have longer schooling to obtain a certificate of some value. It is a risky road, one for which the dangers have already been spelled out by the experience of the American secondary school and the value of the high school diploma. One may even think of this alternative as a cheating form of equality: Everyone is equally entitled to credentials that have lost their value. Guaranteed college graduation does not solve the paradox—the search for equality defeating its own purpose when it is carried to the point of equal results and statuses (Dahrendorf, 1980). Much of the thrust of the search for equality is to enable people to be freer to choose, which means that institutions and programs must offer a wide range of choices while reducing the barriers that prevent people from having those choices. But equal results, in such forms as automatic passage and uniform certification for all, restrict the opportunities for choice.

Reduction of the Transfer-Terminal Distinction. Another alternative is to reduce the distinction between transfer and terminal as much as possible. Here there are two possibilities. One is to narrow the status gap by enhancing the status of the terminal programs. Community college personnel have worked long and hard at this solution, helped considerably by the specific short-term programs that have high practical returns in well-paying and interesting job placements, for example, fashion designer in New York City or electronic technician in a Massachusetts or California technological complex. Those "life chances" do not look bad, compared to the perceivable returns from a bachelor's degree in English or sociology. But the bulk of terminal programs— centered more at the level of secretarial and mechanical training—are nowhere near that attractive and it remains hard to give them a parity of esteem with what people think a full college education will bring. Prestige ranking of occupations by the general population continues to give sociologists something to analyze, setting limits on how much one can realistically rank the middle-status ones with those of high status.

The second possibility is to blur the distinction, reducing as much as possible the labeling of courses and curricula as transfer and nontransfer, and hence the parallel official and self-labeling of students as on one track or the other. Community colleges have long had courses that serve the double purpose and students who mix the two. There are natural administrative interests within comprehensive schools and colleges to reduce the internal distinctions that divide staff and students, and often raise havoc with morale. Then, too, community colleges have long had the self-interest of wanting to certify who is an appropriate candidate for further education without having clearly designated transfer programs in which the specific courses and course sequences are dictated by the programs and requirements of the four-year institutions.

The transfer-terminal distinction and the meaning of the transfer track have blurred somewhat during the last two decades. Some community colleges manipulate the labeling of courses in order to increase their attractiveness and especially to bolster financial support based on student headcounts in degree-credit courses (Cohen and Lombardi, 1979). Part-time students who come to a college just to take a single course, with no intention of getting credit for it let alone using it toward transferring, are found in transfer courses. "The transfer courses have become discrete. Many students already have baccalaureate degrees and are taking the 'transfer' course in photography to gain access to the darkroom, the 'transfer' course in art to have their paintings criticized, the 'transfer' course in a language so that they can travel abroad" (p. 25). In general, an increasingly diffuse approach to transfer programs has been encouraged by basic trends of the last decade: more part-time, occasional, "non-credit" students; more poorly prepared students — as high as 50 percent of enrollment — with the college staff then having to concentrate on the six Rs of higher education — remedial reading, remedial writing, and remedial arithmetic; more student occupational interest; and a "noncollegiate" drift in community college philosophy toward the organization serving as a community center or even a "community-based" legal entity operating without campuses, full-time faculty, or formal curriculum.

But the blurring of distinctions and meanings has limits beyond which lies a loss of legitimacy of the community college *qua* college. The definitions of college held by the four-year institutions and by the general public still set boundaries and insist on distinctions (that auto repairing is not on a par with history or calculus as a college course.) Again we face an alternative with self-defeating tendencies, one sure to arouse much hostility and stimulate countertrends. The community college will still have to pick and choose among courses as to what is bona fide transfer work and worry about course sequences and the progression of students through them. To eliminate the transfer operations would be to give up a hard-won place in the higher education stream" (Cohen and Lombardi, 1979, p. 27).

Move the Problem to Another Type of College. There remains the most general structural alternative: Eliminate the transfer part of the two-year college, or do away with the community college entirely, or convert two-year into four-year institutions. Then the cooling out function, or one of the above alternatives (slightly modified), would have to occur in a four-year context. After all, most four-year colleges in the U.S. system have relatively open admission, and it need not strain them to open the doors still wider. Some of these institutions have had and still have two-year programs and offer two-year degrees, either terminal or allowing entry to the junior and senior years. Also, two-year programs on the main campus and two years of course work available in extension centers have given even major universities an internal "junior college" operation. And now the increasing competition for students is causing four-year colleges to lower admission barriers and to build the two-year segments.

It is easy to imagine some move in this direction and, amidst the bewildering variety of U.S. postsecondary education, this alternative is surely operative today. But, again, it is not an alternative likely to dominate: the two-year entity is institutionalized and here to stay for the foreseeable future. Then, too, the problems that follow from this alternative are sufficient to block any major development. High among the problems is the reluctance of four-year college and university faculties to support two-year programs and to give them esteem. The evidence has long been in on this point, in the form of the marginal status accorded university extension in the family of university programs and A.A. degrees in B.A.–centered institutions. At the same time the need for short-cycle programs does not lessen. As other advanced industrial societies have been finding out the hard way, in their expansion into mass higher education since 1960, the need steadily grows, from both consumer demands and labor market demands, for a greater differentation of degree levels rather than a dedifferentiation. Thus other countries have been moving toward short-cycle education. They too are impelled to devise more stopping points, as well as more educational avenues. The crucial structural decision is then whether to put the short-cycle programs within institutions committed to longer programs of higher esteem or to give them to a separate set of institutions. There is no evidence that the first choice is the superior one. In fact, if successful programs depend upon faculty commitment, there is a strong argument for separate short-cycle colleges.

In short, the problem that causes colleges to respond with the cooling out effort is not going to go away by moving it inside of other types of colleges. *Somebody* has to make that effort, or pursue its alternatives.

Use and Abuse of the Idea

The idea of cooling out has received considerable attention in the last twenty years. The original journal article, "The 'Cooling-Out' Function in Higher Education" (Clark, 1960a), has been widely reprinted in books of reading in sociology, social psychology, and education. The in books of readings in sociology, social psychology, and education. The term used to name the concept undoubtedly has been eye catching.

Beyond this direct absorption of the idea there have been interesting efforts to extend or revise its use, including the construction of counter or opposite concepts. If students can be cooled out, what about faculty? In an important case study of a new community college in a white ethnic part of Boston, London (1978) argued that the faculty suffered a great gap between their expectations and their reality and had to find ways to console themselves and otherwise handle disappointment. The particular college he studied provided a setting likely to magnify this phenomenon, but, even so, what is starkly revealed in an extreme case can be usefully explored in other cases where it may be more muted and shielded from view. As community college experts know well, the gap between expectations and reality is wide wherever the recruited faculty come from traditional sources and have traditional values and then have to face first-generation college-going students who not only have poor scholastic preparation but want to remain attached to their own traditional values of family and neighborhood.

Then, what about cooling out as applied to particular social categories of students? Moore (1975) interviewed over sixty women in three community colleges and focused attention not on their rechanneling from transfer to terminal curricula but rather on a rechanneling of nontraditional career aspirations for women into traditional choices. In most cases, she reported, the two rechannelings coincided. But not in all, since some original choices were for fields such as data processing that were in the terminal track. Hence she skillfully broadened the use of the idea: "The general concept of cooling out, namely the amelioratory process of lowering and rechanneling aspirations, suits women's career choices as well as it does the transfer process" (p. 580). Her focus on women caused her to explore the role of parents and high school counselors, as well as college counselors and the two-year institutions overall, in pressuring women to move away from choices of nontraditional careers.

Then there is the possible development of reverse concepts; is there a "cooling in" or "warming up" function? There surely is, as community college spokesmen have long maintained. There clearly are students who perform better scholastically than they did in high school and who raise rather than lower their aspirations. They may even begin in a terminal program and are moved by observant personnel or by their own efforts to transfer courses. Baird (1971) explored the aspirations of community college students over time, using survey questionnaire data from twenty-seven colleges, and divided the students into *coolers* (lowered aspirations), *warmers* (increased aspirations), and *stayers* (retained original aspirations). He concluded that "contrary to expectation, cooling out occurred seldom, while warming up was relatively common" (p. 163). He pointed to an interplay between high school and college experiences: that coolers (really "coolees"!) had been encouraged by their high school successes to plan for higher degrees, then ran into academic difficulties in the community college and revised their ambitions downward; that warmers had been led by background and high school experiences to plan lower, then succeeded academically in the community college and revised expectations upward. His research had the advantage of a survey covering a large number of colleges and students (over 2,500). But the differences between the groups were small; the results were confusing and hard to integrate; the data centered on self-reported aspirations; the processes of colleges and the actual experiences of students were not observed; and those who were gone by the end of two years were out of the sample.

Without doubt, the most prevalent abuse of the concept of cooling out has been its confusion with casting out. This abuse is not apparent in the serious research literature. Those who have written on the topic have typically observed most of the essential characteristics of the original conception, but I have personally been exposed to it in dozens of conversations and meetings during the years, in such remarks as "she was cooled out" or "don't cool me out" that are meant to refer to a quiet, even devious, effort to simply get rid of or fail someone. Most social science conceptions are liable to a stretching that becomes distorted as they are popularized. One of the major drawbacks to the cooling out terminology is that its catchiness encourages such distortion, all the more readily allowing the idea to slide toward "pop" usage.

Finally, we have the use and potential abuse of the cooling out process in which it is picked up and used in more general analyses of stratification and inequality in society. Here the community college nearly always comes out as a villain, discriminating against the dispossessed, keeping the poor and the minorities away from four-year colleges and universities by letting them in and cooling them out. If this is so, the argument goes, such colleges are then operating objectively as instrumentalities by which the upper classes dominate and maintain privilege. One then need only add a little suspiciousness and the community college is linked to capitalism—at least to American capitalism—with a strong suggestion of a conspiracy in which capitalists construct community colleges to serve their own interests.

In the most carefully constructed argument of this genre, Karabel (1972) has emphasized the large proportions of lower-income and minority students in community colleges. Hence there is a social class difference in who is subjected to the cooling out process, with the community colleges seen as generally operating to maintain the social class system as it is. Karabel points out at the beginning of his essay that this effect is not necessarily intentional; that the two-year college "*has* been critical in providing upward mobility for many individuals" (p. 526) and that measured academic ability is more important than class background in the U.S. in predicting where one goes to college. The main thrust of the argument goes in a different direction. College standards are seen as a covert mechanism for excluding the poor and minorities, serving to justify universities and colleges "as a means of distributing privilege and of legitimating inequality" (p. 539). The community college is essentially a tracking system that is "class-based," (*passim*)—with all the ambiguity of "based." The effort to promote one- and two-year terminal programs is yet another instance of "submerged class conflict" (pp. 548–552), since officials want it while the students do not. And the whiff of conspiracy is strong: "This push toward vocational training in the community college has been sponsored by a national educational planning elite whose social composition, outlook, and policy proposals are reflective of the interests of the more privileged strata of our society" (p. 552). The cooling out process is implicated in all of this, particularly in helping to legitimate inequality by using academic standards in hidden ways to block the upward mobility of the poor and the minorities.

Since Karabel was interested in reform, he concluded with the question of what to do. He suggests that investing more money would not make much difference; that transforming community colleges into four-year institutions would still leave them at the bottom of the prestige hierarchy; and that making the colleges into vocational training centers alone would simply accentuate tracking. The solution he proposes is the grand one of a socialist reconstruction of the entire society: "The problems of inequality and inequality of opportunity are, in short, best dealt with not through educational reform but rather by the wider changes in economic and political life that would help build a socialist society" (p. 558). However, the experiences of socialist societies around the world have hardly been encouraging in their capacity to improve national systems of higher education, including the provision of equal opportunity.

The other major effort in the inequality context, one less carefully constructed, is Zwerling's book, *Second Best: The Crisis of the Com-*

munity College (1976). At the time he wrote the book, Zwerling was a teacher at Staten Island Community College in New York City. He was angry at virtually every aspect of the community college, especially the one at which he worked, other than the special programs and approaches in which he and a few colleagues invested their efforts. He portrayed the community college as "just one more barrier put between the poor and the disenfranchised and the decent and respectable stake in the social system which they seek" (p. xvii). He took note of cooling out, devoting a chapter to it as the main role of counseling, and concluded that it helps the college maintain the existing system of social stratification. By means of cooling out, the college "takes students whose parents are characterized primarily by low income and low educational achievement and slots them into the lower ranks of the industrial and commercial hierarchy. The community college is in fact a social defense mechanism that resists basic changes in the social structure" (p. xix). In helping to maintain inequality, cooling out, as he portrays it, works all too well.

Again, what to do? In a mishmash of new directions, Zwerling proposes consciousness raising, in which students are taught more about what is happening to them, thus making them angry and leading them into a process of heating up that will replace cooling out. In addition they should be given more experience in the real world that will help them choose a career. Then, too, they can be helped over "the transfer trauma" by visits to Yale and similar classy institutions. In short, a "student-centered approach . . . offers the possibility that the old cooling out may at last be replaced by a new heating up" (p. 206). But in his last chapter, Zwerling leaves behind such tinkering and moves to the sweeping structural conclusion that if we want a less hierarchical society, we have to restructure the entire system of higher education, beginning with the elimination of the community colleges: "At the very least this would mean *the elimination* of junior or community colleges since they are the most class-serving of educational institutions" (p. 251). All students would enter directly into a B.A.-granting school. In addition, state systems should award a systemwide B.A., instead of allowing individual colleges and universities to award their own degrees of widely different prestige. All this would eliminate "second best," as everyone moved through equated institutions and obtained equal results.

Arguments of this nature have helped fuel an attack on community colleges by those who single-mindedly pursue the value of equality. Those who speak for minority groups are bound to take a dim view of community colleges and demand direct and open access for whole segments of the population to four-year colleges and universities, when they come to believe that "educational equity means nothing if it does not mean equality of educational attainment" (Winkler, 1977, p. 8).

They then argue that the concern with equality in higher education should shift from getting minority students into colleges to getting them out as graduates holding bachelor's, doctor's, and professional degrees. Any elimination along the way by means of cooling out, dropping out, or flunking out is then suspect as discriminatory, unless it happens in equal portions across social categories.

This shift in the inequality line of reasoning in the U.S. has been little informed by the experiences of national systems elsewhere. Some other nations, particularly France and Italy, have long tried to achieve equal results by means of equated institutions, nationally mandated core and common curricula, and the awarding of degrees by a system-at-large rather than the individual institution. Many systems have long held out against short-cycle institutions and programs, as second best to the traditional universities. But the problems thereby created, as systems moved from elite to mass higher education, have been immense, dwarfing our own in magnitude and making us appear fortunate in comparison. Thus the general drift of painful reform in other advanced systems is toward greater differentiation of types of institutions and degree levels, the introduction of short-cycle programs and degrees, more screening in the first year or two and the breakup of the systemwide degree. The dilemma is still there: Either you keep some aspirants out by selection or you admit everyone and then take your choice between seeing them all through, or flunking out some, or cooling out some. The more other systems get involved in mass entry, the more their problems become similar to ours, including the problem of gap between aspiration and scholastic ability, and the more they must get involved in cooling out or must opt for one or more of the alternatives I have presented.

Conclusion

In the hindsight of two decades, what would I change in the original analysis if I had to do it over again? The most important change would be to have distinguished more clearly between effort and effectiveness in the cooling out process. It is one thing to observe the procedures constructed by colleges and the work they put into cooling out operations, and another to ascertain their effect on students, essentially answering the question whether the effort was effective or not. The distinction was a part of my thinking and writing—appearing in such phrases as "when it is effective"—but should have been clearer. Since I was doing an organizational analysis, I concentrated on the effort side. I had a less clear grasp of the effects, since I was not essentially doing an "impact" analysis, spent much less time with students than with counselors and teachers, and did not systematically interview or survey the students for their reactions. A clearer distinction at the outset could have saved some later confusion about the state of the process. I could also have emphasized a point that naturally follows: The process, no matter how well constructed and operated, is not likely to work smoothly. It tends to become problematic, as individuals and groups react to it. This heavily problematic nature has been caught in some later research, such as Baird (1971) and London (1978). My own writings undoubtedly contributed to it, since social actors can learn from the results of social science and adjust behavior accordingly.

Then, too, it probably would have helped to have carried the cooling out process one step further: after students move from transfer to terminal programs, or while they are being asked to do so, they often quickly move from college to a job or some other form of withdrawal. This would have hooked cooling out to the enormous attrition of community colleges and suggested a major two- or three-step flow in the denial of hope, lowering of aspirations, and disengagement. But all this would have blurred the sharp focus of the original argument, and I did not have good data on the process of complete withdrawal. You have to stop somewhere, if you want to keep guesses from overwhelming limited information.

One change that I would make if I were doing the research now instead of twenty years ago would be to either do research on, or introduce a major *caveat* about, regional and state differences. We should not expect 1,000 community colleges to operate closely alike in the U.S. system, since our decentralized structure has given primacy to local and state control for community colleges and hence has subjected them more to local and state variations than to national administered uniformity. Then, too, the American system of higher education overall is the most market oriented of the world's advanced systems, with competition a prime element that causes colleges to be uncommonly sensitive to different clienteles, labor markets, and the actions of other colleges. Thus, research today on community college operations ought to take seriously the possibility of considerable variation. At the least, regional differences should be studied, since among informed observers it is well known that New England is a long way from California. The East remains relatively transfer oriented and standards oriented—a setting where tradition, resources, and vested interests have given primacy to private higher education and a resulting institutional hierarchy in which the community college often appears as fifth best, let alone second best. It is then hard for researchers in Boston, New Haven, or New York to imagine the "California model," which has developed in a context where public higher education has long been dominant, community colleges won legitimacy before World War II, and virtually everybody in the hometown, or on the block—including grandma—has gone by the college to take a course. In that type of setting, the colleges have had middle-class as well as lower-class clienteles, suburban as well as downtown locations, and students who qualified for selective institutions as well as those who did not. Now, during the 1970s, the California-type college has moved another step down the road of openness, toward becoming such a diffuse enterprise that its legitimacy as a college, as earlier indicated, may soon become problematic. In this evolution, sequential transfer work has become a minor item, as a share of the whole, buried under huge enrollments of "single-course" students. The California model is more widespread and influential in the nation than that exemplified in the Northeast.

The change in approach that I would *not* make if I had to do the study over again, then or now, would be to extrapolate from my internal analysis of the community college to grand theories about the role of education in society. This is too easy as armchair sociology and too lacking in detailed analysis of connecting links. We especially lack the information and the capacity in the state of the art to compare situations in which the cooling out process operates and those in which it does not, the latter then offering one of the alternatives set forth above. The trouble with the leap to grand theory is that, poorly grounded in empirical research, it is particularly vulnerable to ideology of various persuasions. It also tempts Large Solutions, by others if not the researcher, that have a wide gamut of unanticipated and often undesired effects, outcomes that may do major damage to the less knowing and less powerful actors who cannot get out of the way. Witness the way that problematic research by James Coleman and Christopher Jencks has been used by political forces against U.S. public schools. Contemporary social science has grave weaknesses in application to social policy, and nowhere more so than in educational matters. One has to tread gently, even upon the cooling out process and its obviously unattractive features.

This side of utopia, academic systems, whether in a socialist or capitalist country, will be, in Erving Goffman's large phrase, a graveyard of hope. The graveyard may be large or small, busy or infrequently used, but it will be present. Only the naive do not recognize that with hope there is disappointment, with success, failure. The settings that lead toward the cooling out effort remain, all the more so as democracies open doors that were formerly closed. Any system of higher education that has to reconcile such conflicting values as equity, competence, and individual choice — and the advanced democracies are so committed — has to effect compromise procedures that allow for some of each. The cooling out process is one of the possible compromises, perhaps even a necessary one.

References

Baird, L. L. "Cooling Out and Warming Up in the Junior College." *Measurement and Evaluation in Guidance,* 1971, *4* (3), 160–171.

Clark, B. R. *Adult Education in Transition: A Study of Institutional Insecurity.* Berkeley: University of California Press, 1956.

Clark, B. R. "The 'Cooling-Out' Function in Higher Education." *The American Journal of Sociology,* 1960a, *65* (6), 569–576.

Clark, B. R. *The Open Door College: A Case Study.* New York: McGraw-Hill, 1960b.

Cohen, A. M., and Lombardi, J. "Can the Community Colleges Survive Success?" *Change,* 1979, *11* (8), 24–27.

Coleman, J. S. *Equality of Educational Opportunity.* Washington, D.C.: U. S. Government Printing Office, 1966.

Dahrendorf, R. *Life Chances: Approaches to Social and Political Theory.* Chicago: University of Chicago Press, 1980.

Furth, D. "Selection and Equity: An International Viewpoint." *Comparative Education Review,* 1978, *22* (2), 259–277.

Goffman, E. "On Cooling the Mark Out: Some Aspects of Adaptation to Failure." *Psychiatry,* 1952, *15* (4), 451–463.

Jencks, C., and others. *Inequality.* New York: Basic Books, 1972.

Karabel, J. "Community Colleges and Social Stratification." *Harvard Educational Review,* 1972, *42* (4), 521–562.

London, H. B. *The Culture of a Community College.* New York: Praeger, 1978.

Moore, K. M. "The Cooling Out of Two-Year College Women." *Personnel and Guidance Journal,* 1975, *53* (8), 578–583.

Winkler, K. J. "Graduation, Not Admissions, Urged as Desegration Focus." *Chronicle of Higher Education,* March 21, 1977, p. 8.

Zwerling, L. S. *Second Best: The Crisis of the Community College.* New York: McGraw-Hill, 1976.

Burton R. Clark is Allan Murray Cartter Professor of Higher Education and professor of sociology at the University of California, Los Angeles.

In looking at the community college movement today,
the visionary critic of 1969 still advises these schools
to give education a central position in their operations.

Dateline '79 Revisited

Arthur M. Cohen

Criticism is the art of accurate identification. The critic examines the phenomenon in order to better describe it, looking at it from different perspectives, trying to determine what it is of itself, how it compares with others of its category.

The critic of the community colleges attempts to identify them accurately. What are they of themselves? Institutions of learning? Agents of social mobility? Participants in the welfare system? Purveyors of dreams? Contributors to community development? He compares them with other educational structures. What is their niche? What do they offer that is not provided by other schools? How do their operations differ?

Few people criticize the community college in those terms. The colleges are relatively new to American education and have not attracted the attention of many serious scholars. Further, genuine criticism is a rare commodity within the field of education in general. The school is a social agency and, if its proponents would maintain its support, they must justify its contribution to social welfare. Close examination of the ideas and practices of the schools may be perceived as inimicable by the staff. In the extreme, these same practitioners may denounce as an attack any commentary falling outside the genre of self-congratulation. Yet the physician is not an enemy when he critizes the patient's habits saying they may be injurious to health. Criticism, accurate identification, can be helpful to institutions as well as to individuals.

When I published *Dateline '79* (Cohen, 1969), I proposed my version of what a community college would look like it if were organized deliberately to cause student learning. Subtitled *Heretical Concepts for the Community College,* the book criticized the colleges for failure to live up to their own ideals. It was the work of a young scholar four years out of graduate school who had read every book and a sizable percent of all the articles about community colleges (not a great chore because the literature in the early 1960s was small). It was written from disappointment that upon examination the reality of the institutions was far short of the rhetoric of their leaders. The criticism was less of the colleges themselves and those who labored within them than it was of the apologists, the hucksters, the shallow purveyors of banal ideas. The criticism was directed toward those who attempted to elevate the community colleges by erecting straw men, who said the colleges were more caring than the research institutions where aloof scholars rejected contact with undergraduates, more educative than the large universities where students were herded into immense lecture halls and taught by teaching assistants, more accessible than four-year schools that rejected students who could not pay or pass entrance exams. True, perhaps, but it takes more than comparison with the worst features of other institutions to justify one's own practices.

College of '79

Setting aside the disillusion, what did the book seek? The thesis of *Dateline '79* was that the community college should fulfill its promise as a teaching-learning institution. It posed the "College of '79," a hypothetical institution centered on instruction, with general education at the core and occupational education, student personnel services, and community education relegated to the periphery. Instruction in the College of '79 was based on varied media. Each course module could be studied through lecture, discussion, independent study, tutorial, programmed, or computer-assisted instruction sections. The calendar was so arrayed that a student who failed to complete a unit of a course in one instructional form could repeat that unit using a different instructional medium in the succeeding weeks. Students registered for each class section through a fully computerized course registration procedure similar to that used by people making credit card purchases. They could exempt any section by examination. Extramural student activities were minimal and there was no counseling outside the classes, no attempt at presenting noncredit or recreational activities to the community.

The faculty were the instructional managers. They worked a year-round, forty-hour week designing and conducting the course sections and preparing and administering the criterion tests. The administrators were facilitators for the faculty. They operated the centralized data-processing system in which student records were kept along with other information essential to college operation, and they maintained budgets and relations with the funding agencies and the public. The College was set on a half-dozen campuses, each with a maximum of 1,000 students. It was assumed that other agencies in the community would take care of occupational education (proprietary schools), basic education (the K–12 system), and transfer payments (the various welfare bureaus).

Curriculum in the College of '79 was composed of four courses: Communications, Sciences, Social Sciences, and Humanities. Each course was of two years' duration; each was cut into between thirty and forty modules of from two to three weeks each; each module had its own specific, measurable learning outcomes. These specific objectives for each course module were designed so that students could drop in and out of school, taking portions of courses at their own pace. But, taken as a whole, the curriculum *was* general education. All students took the four core courses; there were few electives.

The College of '79 was never built; I did not expect it to be built. It was a model with many parts, and some of them were embraced by the community colleges in the 1970s. The idea that instruction in the same courses could be carried on through sections using different media has become widespread. Centralized data processing and ease of student registration is common. Individualized study and credit for experience, other features of the College of '79, have also been adopted. However, some parts of the plan made little headway. The book included a plea for general education but during the 1970s most community colleges moved so far toward occupational education that the liberal arts and sciences were severely attenuated. And the principle that all courses should be based on specific measurable objectives is still articulated but rarely followed in practice.

Dateline '79 foresaw the almost total collapse of curriculum in the community colleges during the 1970s and indeed that happened. Curriculum is a sequence of intended learnings usually packaged into courses. The key phrase in the definition is "sequence of intended learnings." *Sequence* suggests a pattern or progression that has some rationale, order, deliberate arrangement. *Intended learnings* suggests outcomes defined in advance, predictable effects. A curriculum is arranged for students who are expected to follow the sequence of courses. A degree or certificate of completion is typically awarded to testify that a person has followed that sequence.

The 1970s saw the number of degrees and certificates awarded drop precipitously as a percent of the people enrolled. Curriculums are still listed in the catalogues but only a miniscule proportion of the entering students follow those sequences. The idea of individualized study has been interpreted to mean a separate set of goals for every matriculant. In most community colleges now, except for the occupational programs that have a licensure examination at their culmination, students attend what courses they will and in whatever sequence they choose. If social justice demands that each individual achieve some form of success in college, and if the idea of education is interpreted to mean that all people may use the college to strive toward idiosyncratic intentions, the curriculum explodes. Courses rise and fall according to the whims of the clientele. That happened in the community colleges in the 1970s. That will happen in any school that purports to serve up anything that anyone in the community wants.

Dateline '79 also predicted that the course as the basic unit of instruction would not survive either. That is why the book postulated learning modules, each with its own specified objectives, criterion tests, and media. And in practice, community college course integrity has been violated. A recent study of students in California community colleges suggests that a sizable proportion of the students leave before completing their courses because they have learned what they wanted and they have no need for institutionally awarded credits (Hunter and Sheldon, 1979). Others leave because they have become disaffected with the instructors or because something more attractive has gained their attention. They know they can return at any time; in the Chicago City Colleges a student may not be dismissed from a course for lack of attendance. Nationwide the grade of *W,* issued to students who fail to complete a course in the allotted time, has become commonplace.

Dateline '79 was critical but it did not engender a succession of works similarly critical of community college curriculum and instruction. During the past ten years the literature has changed but slightly. Still with us are the putative Marxists who see a capitalist conspiracy behind every classroom door. They feel certain the community colleges were erected only to keep the downtrodden masses in their place by giving them the illusion of access to higher education while denying them entrance to the prestigious institutions where real social class movement is found. Still with us are the hucksters, the expansionists who want ever-more students, funds, and programs. To them, growth is the *sine qua non,* and the truly successful community college is one that has aggregated unto itself all the occupational, adult, lower-division, and remedial education in its district along with a full complement of community services.

Many who write about the colleges tend not to realize that they are schools and should be so judged. To them, evidence of learning attained by the students is less important than student satisfaction with the experience. They see the colleges only peripherally as educative institutions, choosing instead to view them as agents of transfer payments, of upward mobility for individuals, as shock absorbers for disenfranchised groups demanding entrance to higher education as recreational and cultural centers for the community, or as credentialing agencies certifying people for employment.

And yet, taking all these writers together still leaves a paucity of synthesizers. Most people who write about these institutions see a part as the whole. They discuss programs and take positions of advocacy for various curriculums. Or they find categories of students who are underrepresented in the institutions and argue for vigorous recruitment efforts among these populations. The effects of different types of programs or new groups of students on overall institutional functioning are rarely considered.

Setting aside the commentary on *Dateline '79* but staying within its scope, it is instructive to plot trends for community colleges in the 1980s. The unintended consequences of several widely acclaimed innovations have now become apparent. Nonpunitive grading was adopted because we did not want to jeopardize the academic career of people who had failed in courses taken at an earlier time. But the W grades led to severe grade inflation as instructors began awarding them instead of Ds and Fs (McCuen, 1978). The policies of withdrawal without penalty at any time prior to the end of the term also contributed to a casual approach to studies on the part of students who began dropping courses capriciously. And during the 1970s responsibility for the curriculum and for instructional media was assigned increasingly to administrators who could presumably allocate resources better in response to community and legislative demands. But this effectively removed control of the curriculum from faculty hands, led to greater faculty isolation, and enhanced the faculty move for countervailing power.

Certain practices imminent for the 1980s may likewise lead to untoward results. The colleges seem determined to maintain enrollments despite fewer people in the eighteen- to twenty-one-year-old age group and a lower rate of participation in higher education in general. The inexorable facts of demography point to a lessened demand for institutional services. The number of people completing high school has been reduced. The colleges are engaged in competition with other educational structures for the shrinking pool of potential students. They think they serve nontraditional students, older students, returning women, and the other categories of new students best with similarly new programs without realizing there is a limit to the number and extent of quasi-educational activities that the people of a community will support.

It is possible to salvage enrollments without compromising the educative integrity of the institution, for example, by rescheduling classes in a fashion to better fit the students' schedules apart from school. Some success has been achieved by institutions that have switched their basic transfer courses from the one-hour-a-day, Monday-Wednesday-Friday schedule to a three-hour, one-day-a-week pattern. Most students take only one or two courses a term anyway, and scheduling those courses in three-hour blocks makes it easier for the commuter students to fit work schedules around them and saves travel expense in getting to the campus. But the colleges do less of that, more of the recreational and human service activities that fall perilously close to being noneducative functions. They fail to appreciate the fact that it is possible for a market — any market — to become saturated, especially if the purveyors are presumed to be in a different business.

Community colleges enter the 1980s with expectations that, as they tap new markets, their efforts in career, compensatory, and community education will be supported by ever-growing enrollments. They may do well in comparison with certain other sectors of postsecondary education but there are some warning signals, some indicators that the way may not be smooth. Full-time baccalaureate-bound students may be lost to those senior institutions that reduce entry requirements and recruit aggressively. Adult part-time enrollments may fail to grow because of saturation of demand and because peoples' volitional expenditures for education may change. Community services are increasingly being put on a pay-as-you-go basis. There is also some indication that the public may be disinclined to support remedial education at the college level, feeling that they have already paid for people to learn the three Rs in the lower schools. And since the community colleges grew rapidly in the 1960s as a result of their taking the overflow from senior institutions, when there is no overflow, the reasons for their growth become less pronounced. If the colleges acted as the lungs of the system in the 1960s, expanding when additional students clamored for entry, so now they must contract in the 1980s when the senior institutions will stand ready to accept all comers.

As for curriculum in the 1980s, the colleges will tend to continue to present the liberal arts exclusively through the transfer courses as though they were suited only for students who seek baccalaureate degrees. Are they only for an elite group that has time to spend on frills and in leisure pursuits? The faculty seem unable to make the essential conversions that would restructure the liberal arts so that they fit the career and compensatory education programs that are being maximized in their colleges. They also seem unwilling to address the broader issues of community life through the liberal arts in noncredit offerings. Yet rapid change is essential if the liberal arts are to survive in more than miniscule form.

During the 1980s the colleges will continue emphasizing the three Cs: career, compensatory, and community education. They have established a stronghold on occupational education with more than half their students enrolled in courses and curricula leading to immediate employment. Recertification and relicensure will become requirements in more occupations, hence the colleges will maintain their programs and courses in which members of various occupational groups continue their education. Compensatory or remedial studies will be maintained as the community colleges are seen as adult education centers and as the point of first entry for immigrants who need language skills and entry level occupational preparation. Community education will thrive, but on a pay-as-you-go basis. The community colleges will probably be forced to split off their community service divisions as the universities did their extension centers.

Still, because the forces propelling different types of people into the community colleges operate at varying rates of speed, community colleges in some areas will take distinct forms. Even now, in some states the community colleges have primary responsibility for adult basic education, while in others that function remains with the public schools; and some states have devised community colleges as technical institutes with the liberal arts presented only through the university branches. This differentiation may lead to distinct types of community colleges such as the following.

Resurrected Secondary School. In areas where the demand for access to traditional forms of postsecondary education remains high, the community college may take a form similar to that of the contemporary secondary school. Here the faculty will see themselves as job holders having minimal contact with the administrators. The administrators will function primarily as interpreters of education codes. The campuses will be fenced-in enclaves with guards at the gate and in every corridor. The curriculum will be based on the three Rs plus numerous courses in job-getting skills and entry level occupational competencies. Schooling may be all but compulsory as young people find they cannot work even at entry level jobs without some sort of certificate issued by a postsecondary institution.

Broker. The pattern of educational organization in some areas may propel community colleges into becoming brokers for other agencies. These colleges would accept as students people who were referred from welfare bureaus and unemployment agencies when their entitlements ran out. They would attempt to teach entry level skills but their primary function would be as agents of transfer payments, continuing the award of benefits to people who for whatever reason were not otherwise employed. They would also link their clients with other schools more suited for their purposes, paying the tuition for students who would attend proprietary schools and private colleges in the region. They would award credit for experience and otherwise certify their clients as having certain competencies. Their main functions would be to counsel their students, find jobs or other educational structures for them, and support them while they are in transition stages in their life.

Rapid Response College. Another form of community college might be the rapid response institution, the college that devises short courses and presentations in response to community demands. The closest approximations to those types of institutions currently are the colleges without campuses: Coastline Community College in California, Whatcom Community College in Washington, and the Community College of Vermont, among others. These institutions would have no permanent faculty, employing only those people who would teach courses part time and on an ad hoc basis. They would be operated by a cadre of instructional development designers who would seek out areas of current interest and arrange courses to fit them. Open-circuit television broadcasts, cultural and recreational functions, and activities patterned to fit immediate community interest would be the vehicle through which these institutions would serve their clients. No college credits would be awarded; it would remain for the more traditional certifying institutions in the community to determine whether participants in the rapid response colleges' programs had learned.

Certification Center. One type of community college might operate exclusively as a certification center designed solely for occupational training and licensure. It would have extensive shops and laboratories of its own and would lease other facilities in its surrounding area in which students would be prepared for trades. Its managers would seek students from occupational groups whose members needed or were forced to gain supplemental skills. It would act as an academy for the police and fire fighters, the training center for the paramedics and the nurses' aides. It would prepare automobile mechanics, restaurant workers, airline attendants. All would be done without the pretext of the institution as a college parallel school preparing people for baccalaureate degrees.

Satellite Center. Where the community colleges maintain responsibility for most of the lower-division education in their region, the colleges may take the form of small autonomous campuses. Each center would be responsible for devising its own curriculum. The district office would maintain fiscal control but the campus staff would offer those courses that best suit the preferences of the people in their neighborhood and would maintain their own articulation agreements with the senior institutions. There might be a small corps of full-time staff members and numerous paraprofessional aides, much reproducible media. The campuses would be managed by a provost selected from the ranks of the people operating the center. The curriculum would be founded on general education and on the personal interests of the local populace.

All these scenarios suggest a form of local control. But the trend toward state control may continue and become so pronounced that by 1990 few colleges will maintain their local autonomy. Then the multi-institution district will be the norm with the single college serving a large region or an entire state through numerous campuses and local centers. The pretext of individual colleges will disappear; the college president would become a campus head and the college organization form would not be seen. Budgeting, instructional planning, employment of personnel, and curriculum design all would be done in the central office. An astute, powerful administration would maintain a far-flung agency.

The community colleges have succeeded in their intent to open the way to higher education for the masses. Wherever they exist access is easy. Anyone who wants to attend may; there are few barriers. But success breeds expectations. An educational system that teaches reading, for example, leads to demands that all people learn to read. When it then passes people through who have not learned to read, the system is seen to have failed. Witness the criticism of the public schools currently. Similarly a college offering degrees that lead to lucrative employment generates expectations that all people who receive its degrees will gain better jobs. And people seeking to elevate their social class will demand admission to the institution that promises to propel its graduates into higher-status positions within the society. When they graduate and find their relative income and social status unchanged, they may feel they have been cheated. Witness the attacks on higher education.

The budget for education will be a central battleground in the 1980s. The community colleges must compete for dollars with other public agencies: welfare bureaus, parks and recreation services, police and fire departments, prisons and parole bureaus. Can the colleges maintain their funds? They will need increased budgets because the ravages of inflation and negotiated contracts will lead to continual increases in the cost of instruction without complementary gains in productivity. The 1970s did not bring the financial savings that were promised by the proponents of reproducible media. Some funds were saved through the use of hourly-rate part-time instructors, but that avenue may be closed as the faculty organizations grow stronger. Quality instruction is expensive and the more community colleges attempt to educate the students of lesser ability, the more expensive that instruction will be.

For their own sake, community colleges would do well to restore the educative dimension to a central position in their operations during the 1980s. Although their programs are based ostensibly on instruction, too few students complete programs or courses and too few learn much that the college purports to have taught. Sizable programs have been developed to serve people referred by unemployment offices and welfare bureaus. Sizable numbers of students attend primarily for the fiscal benefits accruing to them through the various channels of student aid. The colleges cannot afford to be perceived as agents of the welfare system.

Institutional legitimacy is compromised to the extent the colleges tend away from their basic educational functions. Notwithstanding all the calls for new missions, the colleges must be instructional enterprises. The public may take dimly the idea of supporting an institution in which people attend but do not complete any program. Put another way, "It is unreasonable to expect that the institutions will continue to be supported indefinitely without clearer definition of their effects on students and their contributions to community life." And that is where *Dateline '79* began.

References

Breneman, D. W. "Planning as if People Mattered: The Economy." Presentation to the 14th annual conference, Society for College and University Planning, Kansas City, Mo., July 9, 1979.

Cohen, A. M. *Dateline '79: Heretical Concepts for the Community College.* Beverly Hills: Glencoe Press, 1969.

Hunter, R., and Sheldon, M. S. *Statewide Longitudinal Study. Report on Academic Year 1978–1979. Part I, Fall Results.* Woodland Hills, Calif.: Pierce College, 1979. 86 pp. ED 180 530.

McCuen, J. T., and others. *Report of the Commission on Academic Standards.* Los Angeles: Los Angeles Community College District, 1978. 53pp. ED 160 176.

Arthur M. Cohen is professor of higher education at the University of California at Los Angeles and director of the ERIC Clearinghouse for Junior Colleges.

*Critics claim that community colleges reinforce
class status and privilege. The author suggests that the
colleges could be part of an alternative system of
higher education, equal in quality but different in kind
from traditional four-year schools.*

Community Colleges: Alternative to Elitism in Higher Education

J. Richard Johnston

Surveying the turbulent campus scene in the 1960s, John Gardner remarked that American higher education was caught between uncritical lovers and unloving critics. Although interpretive evaluation is central to the process of education, American colleges and universities do not take kindly to criticism and, according to Cohen (1969), that applies particularly to the community college. "Instead of genuine self-appraisal, most of its writings contain a curious mixture of defensiveness and self-congratulation" (p. viii).

Ten years ago Cohen's *Dateline '79: Heretical Concepts for the Community College* sketched a futuristic view of the colleges. Whatever other changes occurred in the intervening decade, increased receptivity to criticism was not one of them. At the 1979 meeting of the American Association of Community and Junior Colleges in Chicago, Illinois, Steven Zwerling analyzed the role of the colleges along the lines of themes developed in his book *Second Best*. The reaction of the college administrators in attendance to Zwerling's critical workshop presentation was mostly defensive and even hostile, one administrator rising to say publicly at the close of the session, "I think Mr. Zwerling is second best."

If, as Socrates believed, the unexamined life is not worth living, we might speculate that in this period of rapid social change the unexamined institution cannot long endure. In undertaking such an examination we would first insist that the community college is an integral part of American higher education. Colleges and universities in America have accepted the responsibility for certain functions some of which are not complementary to one another and others of which may indeed be incompatible. Four of the most frequently mentioned tasks of higher education are: (1) searching for new knowledge while training researchers to maintain scientific and cultural inquiry; (2) training professional practitioners; (3) transmitting culture; and (4) providing services to the community on a local, regional, or national scale.

The problems of integrating such a diversity of purposes into one unified academic institution are many. Basic research to extend knowledge and applied research (or technology) are not easily coordinated with one another; neither are they easily coordinated with the tasks of promoting literacy, teaching effective study skills, or bolstering self-confidence in a growing clientele. This is especially true when this clientele includes many first-generation-college students from families and social groups which look to the colleges to act simultaneously as therapeutic institutions, purveyors of culture, and job placement specialists. Providing services to the community, often on a client or contract basis for consulting or research, and transmitting culture are not necessarily complementary functions. They often involve choices that are essentially political; for example, setting up research valuable for agribusiness or teaching organizational theory to migrant workers.

As higher education expanded, the need for parallel programs and alternative institutions became apparent. The land-grant colleges, some agricultural and technical universities, and a few postsecondary technical schools did not suffice to appease the American appetite for higher learning. Thus the two-year college came into being, first as a junior college principally for liberal arts transfer students and, after World War II, as a comprehensive community college.

The community colleges serve a broader cross section of the population than traditional colleges and provide a greater variety of programs, ranging from liberal arts associate degree curricula through the training of paraprofessional technicians to basic literacy and educational services for groups with particular needs — the elderly, women, the handicapped and the like.

The goals of community colleges are (1) to offer a comprehensive curriculum including transfer or college parallel courses (equivalent to lower-level undergraduate work at a traditional liberal arts college), technical-vocational programs (to teach skills leading to employment immediately upon completion) or terminal occupational courses;

(2) to practice an open-door admissions policy making the colleges accessible to all adult citizens whether or not they have finished high school; (3) to provide instruction in convenient locations to a commuter population who can combine part-time work with full-time study, or vice versa; (4) to give early school-leavers and unsuccessful learners from all social groups and age categories a second chance in the educational system; and (5) to be responsive to the local needs of the community and provide intellectual and cultural leadership in meeting a variety of community needs. In sum, the goals of the colleges are to make higher education accessible to the mass of people.

In addition to the goals listed above, some observers see the colleges as having other objectives that constitute a hidden agenda (or curriculum). Various critics list these goals as follows: (1) to "cool out" students of low ability or deficient academic background, thus protecting selective elitist institutions; (2) to sort and filter students along class lines, thus perpetuating working class and underprivileged groups—the proletariat in Marxist terms—in their lower-class status; (3) to train a paraprofessional work force at public expense for the private profit of local industry; and (4) to provide a custodial function for unemployed youth by offering a debased education which is essentially an extension of high school study in the guise of college curriculum.

Criticism of Community Colleges

Goffman (1952) analyzed the way society handles persons whose expectations have been blocked or frustrated and whose self-concepts have been shattered. In such situations a person must accept an involuntary change of social roles or status which requires the surrender of old values and a commitment to the concept of self and different values which the new role requires or allows. "A person may be involuntarily deprived of his position or involvement and made in return something that is considered a lesser thing to be" (p. 454). Borrowing from the terminology of the underworld of gambling, Goffman describes this process as "cooling out the mark" (p. 452). In essence cooling out the mark is providing an acceptable adaptation to failure.

Clark (1960) later used *cooling out* to refer to the way community colleges divert expectations of a student from the glories of professional life as a college graduate to the rewards and advantages of vocational preparation for immediate employment. The mark—in this case the student—is led to lower his or her expectations and accept an inferior role or status as a nonprofessional worker or indeed to drop out entirely without excessive resentment, feeling that he or she has had a fair chance and failed.

According to this view, by accepting the less motivated, less competent, and often poorly prepared students, the colleges relieve the pressure on more selective institutions. This enables elitist colleges to maintain and reinforce the social status of the privileged classes in our society.

Karabel (1974, p. 14) describes this function: "So everyone had a chance to attend college somewhere but, more critically the elite institutions remained undefiled by the masses demanding access . . . .Thus the community college, seemingly the very expression of a democratic system of higher education, protects the portals of elite institutions." This permits elitist institutions to use academic standards as a mechanism to perform the dubious function of distributing privilege by certifying and legitimating inequality.

There are those who see community colleges functioning to sort and filter students along class lines to perpetuate economically underprivileged groups — the real proletariat — in their lower-class status. While similar to the cooling out process, this is a more generalized function. "As the numbers increase and a vocational track is created, higher status institutions must be made even more selective. In this way . . . you get them coming and going" (Zwerling, 1976, p. 69).

As a sorting mechanism the two-year colleges not only discourage those not destined for further education by placing them in a terminal program or flunking them out, but they also encourage the able and motivated individuals among the nontraditional students to enter transfer programs or to qualify for technical and semiprofessional jobs.

In this sorting process the two-year colleges constitute the lowest track of higher education. They are "in reality a prime contemporary expression of the dual historical pattern of class-based tracking and educational inflation . . . . An analysis of the existing evidence will show that the community college is itself the bottom track of the system of higher education both in class origins and occupational distribution of its students. Further, tracking takes place *within* the community college in the form of vocational education" (Karabel, 1972, p. 526). Karabel sees this as a class-based tracking system sifting working class students out of the educational system or diverting them to low pay and low-status jobs. He feels that if the colleges were truly a democratizing force in our society, they would tend to modify the American class structure by helping to redistribute income and social status.

In addition, some commentators would say that community colleges are being used to train a paraprofessional work force at public expense for the private profit of local industry. The category of technical and professional worker is a rapidly growing sector of the labor force. Four-year colleges and universities train the majority of these workers. Community colleges have the specific task of training the technical or paraprofessional workers, who need more than a high school education but less than a bachelor's degree, to assist the professional worker.

This lowering of career expectations is a psychological aspect of cooling out as well as a way of screening to get future hewers of wood and carriers of water for an industrial society. "The terminal student can be made to appear not so radically different from the transfer student, e.g., an 'engineering aide' instead of 'engineer,' and hence he goes to something with a status of his own. This reflects less unfavorably on a person's capacities" (Clark, 1960, p. 164). The process also recruits for the local labor force, training people for jobs requiring only two years of college, including teachers' aides, x-ray technicians and computer operators. Thus community college graduates will enter lower-paying jobs that have less job satisfaction and fewer chances for mobility than graduates of more selective four-year liberal arts colleges. And local industry is spared the cost of training workers to fill specific job slots.

In other words, instead of enhancing the range and quality of options available to nontraditional students who seek learning and social advancement, the community colleges tend to limit educational opportunity by channeling students into specialized training for specific low-status jobs.

Some critics claim that community colleges provide programs for low-achieving students in order to keep these young people out of the labor market, off the streets, and out of trouble. The availability of tuition-free or low-cost colleges for local students serves to prolong dependency and extend adolescence by encouraging many young students to remain at home. According to Jencks and Riesman, "The gradual extension of adolescence has already produced a variety of problems America cannot handle satisfactorily; universal junior college would make the situation appreciably worse" (1968, p. 56).

Because many of the early two-year colleges were tied to high schools from which many of their faculty and administrators were recruited and because of their unfavorable position in recruiting academically talented faculty during the period of phenomenal growth through the sixties into the early seventies these colleges reflect secondary school attitudes frequently manifesting a populist aversion to anything smacking of academic elitism. Jencks and Riesman discussed this in a chapter entitled "The Anti-University College."

Concern for the leveling influence of the colleges is not limited to the dilution of lower-division studies and academic degrees. Educators like Meyerson (1975) have been concerned that growing financial support for the colleges and the establishment of uniform salary scales for college professors would also have a negative impact on academic quality. Speaking of a City of New York union contract creating a single salary scale, he wrote that this "egalitarian remuneration makes little distinction between levels of teaching, research, or merit . . . . The monolithic approach to faculty remuneration has a leveling effect; it's difficult to maintain quality when rewards are not made selectively" (p. 310). Elsewhere in the article Meyerson says, "If the basic structure of the system is to be arranged so that contingencies work only to the advantage of the less-favored institutions, there will be downward leveling. It seems clear that general equalization of budgets and salaries as well as admissions will lead to mediocrity" (p. 313).

Such views support arguments that there is a similar tracking system for professors through a differential system of rewards whereby the elite schools pay their more meritorious faculty better salaries than community college faculty, who are presumably less meritorious.

Much of the criticism of two-year colleges published in the past two decades suffers from a tendency toward overgeneralization about diverse institutions; then, too, the role of transfer students has been exaggerated. Critics of the colleges as a mechanism for sorting students on the basis of social class have relied heavily upon statistics showing that the majority of students were enrolled in transfer programs and that a relatively small percentage succeeded in earning academic degrees. As we enter the decade of the 1980s, enrollment patterns have radically shifted, with a majority of students enrolled in career programs. Some four-year liberal arts college graduates returning for technical job training are among the large number of adults who, by enrolling on a part-time basis at an older age, are changing the profile of community college students.

All of this does not invalidate the conclusion that the colleges reinforce class stratification, but the burden of empirical proof that this is a deliberate policy rests upon those who advance the argument. It seems to me that a theoretical interpretation of the community college as a capitalistic weapon against the working classes is somewhat simplistic when it attributes a great unity of purpose, if not a conspiratorial design, to institutions which have developed in response to a variety of demands—demands which grow out of ambiguous but real yearnings for a democratic society providing a large measure of equality.

Nevertheless we should not dismiss out-of-hand the argument that community colleges contribute to social stratification or that they enhance the privileged position of those in the community who already have higher levels of education, social status, and income than those with the most need for further education. The nearest thing we have to a proletariat in Marxist terms—minorities, rural poor, unskilled blue-collar workers, unemployed urban youth, women of all ages from the poorest groups in our society—have not attended college in numbers commensurate with their proportion of the population. The colleges have tended to reinforce class privileges by failing to help these groups as well as by encouraging others to emphasize job training rather than education.

One need not accept the theory that a hierarchical power structure reinforces class privilege by manipulating students in order to understand why open admission and low-cost colleges attract minorities and the poor. By some estimates more than half of all blacks who do attend college are in two-year colleges; these schools also attract Spanish-speaking and other minorities, most of whom share the characteristic of being poor. In fact, the enrollments of the colleges in large urban centers reflect and probably reinforce various kinds of segregation along the lines of race, ethnicity, and income.

Community colleges need not be apologetic about training workers for local firms so long as this does not detract from the global mission of the institution. In meeting its own needs and promoting its own interests local industry has a legitimate claim upon the colleges. There are large areas of cooperation where the interests of students and general public are served through work-study and other programs that provide workers for industry and valuable learning experiences for students. But it would be unfortunate if the community college minimized its role as intellectual analyst, social critic, and protector of the public interest, something which is much broader than and sometimes in conflict with the interests of private firms and public corporations which provide most of the jobs available in the community.

Alternative System of Higher Education

A technological society needs a variety of educational institutions capable of preparing postsecondary students and other adults to assume productive social roles ranging from semiskilled workers to research scientists. Selective colleges and universities perform useful functions as centers of theoretical investigation and basic research. But why should we not build alternative systems to produce a genuine diversity of institutions in higher education rather than a hierarchy that parallels existing social class divisions? Why should not the great majority of workers be encouraged to complete the bachelor of arts degree or an equivalent amount of study and even beyond? Why should the practical nurse, the library technician and the dental hygienist not aspire to graduate-level studies to achieve a more comprehensive view of themselves and their work in a more universal setting?

If the community colleges are to be a major part of an alternative system of higher education, rather than serving as educational service institutions responding to various uncoordinated community needs, they will have to address the question of what their roles should be in terms of broad purposes and social goals. A technological society needs skilled workers. There are jobs to be filled, and the training of workers to perform useful labor is a necessary function. One can argue that this function is not incompatible with an education, which also awakens critical faculties and promotes individual personal growth in terms of developing human potential. But this latter view basically challenges the existing system of social stratification and is not consistent with the prevailing opinion that we should avoid producing overqualified degree holders who may become a source of social and political discontent.

What would an alternative system of higher education look like? What would be its constituent parts and how would they function?

An alternative system might consist of community colleges, cooperating senior institutions, selected technical schools, and a network of learning opportunities in industry and government. These components could constitute a system equal in quality to but different in kind from traditional four-year liberal arts colleges and universities.

An alternative system of learning networks would rely less heavily upon formal classroom instruction than traditional colleges while emphasizing experiential learning, independent study, and the demonstration of competency by whatever means achieved. Counseling would play an important role in helping individual students to devise learning strategies consistent with their own life experiences, learning styles, and career goals. Students should be encouraged to develop a broad philosophical view of the social, cultural, and intellectual significance of the knowledge they acquire and the technical skills they master.

Evaluation and certification procedures will be crucial elements in developing an alternative system. Along with the evaluation of work and study experiences and the demonstration of competency, new kinds of testing instruments should be devised—the College Level Examination Program and the New York Regents proficiency examinations are examples—to evaluate prior learning. Evaluation of student achievement, while different, may be more rigorous than the present system of writing papers and passing tests to collect course credits. The community colleges should develop alternative credentials that will certify levels of skills and competency and enjoy a parity of esteem with liberal arts degrees now awarded on the basis of time served and credits accumulated.

The mission of such a system would be to enhance the range and quality of options available to students in search of learning beyond secondary studies on an open-admissions basis. The system must be more comprehensive than a collection of occupational training programs teaching specialized skills; it must also provide general education to bring the cultural heritage into contact with the everyday life of students.

An integral feature of higher education has been a core of studies intended to create a desire for further growth as complete human beings on the part of students and to provide them with the means to advance toward the fulfillment of such desires. Traditionally the liberal arts have claimed to do this. Perhaps the most significant development of community colleges in the past few years is the erosion of the transfer function in offering university parallel courses in the liberal arts. According to statistics of the Illinois Community College Board, only a small proportion of all credit-course students — about 5 percent in Illinois — transfer to senior institutions as degree candidates. The movement of the colleges is away from liberal arts and transfer programs toward remedial studies, occupational curricula, and specialized community services.

Diverse and difficult are the problems of combining liberal studies and career training in a system of education for the masses. An alternative system of higher education, which includes the community colleges, must find a way to finance remedial education, which is expensive, and a means of integrating it into the total curriculum; it must determine the role of liberal studies in order to provide a philosophical foundation so that all programs including occupational studies contribute to further growth rather than limiting learning to specific job skills; and it must maintain legitimacy as a system of higher education in the eyes of a public accustomed to judging (and supporting) educational institutions according to the status conferred by their degrees as well as the learning stimulated by their programs of study.

No system of education that ignores the economic organization of society and its needs for special work skills can expect to enjoy popular support. Conversely, no system of education that ignores the needs of people for personal development and human fulfillment, which does not recognize education as an end in itself and does not view humanity as our most valuable natural resource, can enjoy the status of higher education. The creation of such a system is the challenge that community colleges must meet if they are to assume a role of leadership in providing a genuine alternative to a selective system of colleges and universities.

References

Cohen, A. M. *Dateline '79: Heretical Concepts for the Community College.* Beverly Hills: Glencoe Press, 1969.

Clark, B. R. *The Open Door College: A Case Study.* New York: McGraw-Hill, 1960.

Goffman, E. "On Cooling the Mark Out: Some Aspects of Adaptation to Failure." *Psychiatry,* 1952, *15* (4), 451–463.

Jencks, C., and Riesman, D. *The Academic Revolution* New York: Doubleday, 1968.

Karabel, J. "Protecting the Portals: Class and the Community College." *Social Policy,* 1974, *5* (1), 12–18.

Karabel, J. "Community Colleges and Social Stratification." *Harvard Educational Review,*
1972, *42* (4), 521–562.

Meyerson, M. "Quality and Mass Education." *Daedalus,* 1975, *104* (1), 304–321.

Zwerling, L. S. *Second Best: The Crisis of the Community College.* New York: McGraw-Hill,
1976.

J. Richard Johnston is editor of Community College Frontiers.

*Despite multiple challenges, some community college students
transfer to and graduate from four-year schools. The community
college experience is crucial to their success.*

The Community College Elite

William Neumånn
David Riesman

Anyone familiar with American higher education will be struck by the
paradox in the title of this essay. The terms *community college* and *elite*
seem an unlikely combination. The conventional perception of community colleges is that neither the institutions nor their students are in
any way elite. Yet there are relatively small, but significant, numbers
of community college students who transfer to selective independent
colleges and universities, that is, to what many consider the elite institutions. More specifically, these students would not have been admitted to these selective institutions as freshmen, but they are admitted
because of their community college performance. It is this group of students who are admitted to selective independent four-year institutions,
reach four-year status, and graduate whom we identify as the community
college elite. The community college elite may be described as nontraditional students who follow an unconventional path to the independent senior institutions.

We are indebted for financial support of our research to the Exxon Education
Foundation, the Carnegie Council on Policy Studies in Higher Education and The Per-
anent Charity Fund of Boston.

It is dangerous to generalize about community colleges since, as one of us has hypothesized earlier, "There is as much variety among community colleges as there is among four-year institutions" (Riesman, 1978, p. 1). There are also very clear regional differences to consider. There is, no doubt, less stigma attached to attending one of the 106 community colleges in California than there is to attending one of the 18 community colleges in Massachusetts. Within the ranks of community colleges there are those institutions which are identified as the elite and, as we have found, there are elite students in all the community colleges, yet the public perception of community colleges as being generally inferior to four-year institutions persists.

Although Astin (1975, 1977) has found in his continuing surveys that students in community colleges tend to be more satisfied with the curriculum, including its science program, than those at four-year colleges, and although there is a good deal of evidence in California that those who do transfer from community colleges to one of the campuses of the University of California system do better than the students who began in these same institutions (in part because of superior teaching at the lower-division level), it also is probably true, as Clark (1960) argued long ago, that some students are "cooled out" of transfer programs in community colleges. Astin (1977, p. 247) maintains that the general lack of residential facilities and the low student involvement in campus life are among the reasons why students' chances of persisting to the baccalaureate are "less at a two-year college than at a four-year college, public or private," especially for those going on directly from high school. Given the sometimes tenuous connections of community college students to their institutions, what is lacking is national data on numbers of community college transfer students, many of whom have stopped out of one institution and started again in another. This has been discussed by Cohen (1979), who suggests that it will be some time before an accurate count can be made. We cannot today assume that the transfer programs are the ones where cooling out is most required, because it is often the terminal vocational programs that are selective (especially if there is any kind of science requirement, or if, as in nursing programs, facilities are tight), with transfer programs attracting the generally less-motivated students. The purpose of this essay is not to respond to, let alone add to, all the criticisms made of community colleges for supposedly stratifying students and placing a ceiling on their aspirations. It is to seek to understand how it has come about that in Massachusetts, where there are only eighteen community colleges—most of which did not exist before 1970—with the relatively small total enrollment of 69,789, several hundred students have in the past few years managed the transition to independent four-year colleges and universities. Some of these students transferred to the most selective institutions in the country—and the large majority of these students then obtained the baccalaureate.

This is a self-selected elite not actively recruited by institutions, many of which have such tiny attrition they have little room for transfers. To understand how these particular students beat the odds, we conducted intensive interviews with community college transfer students at a number of the selective institutions. The interviews were open ended but focused on the students' educational experiences; essentially, we collected educational life histories.

As a group, these students share many of the characteristics of the "new students" described by Cross. "Most of these students were Caucasian whose fathers work or worked at blue-collar jobs. Most of the parents have never attended college, and expectation of college is new to the family. The new students themselves have not been especially successful at their school studies. Whereas traditional college students (upper third) have made As and Bs in high school, new students have made mostly Cs. Traditional students are attracted primarily to four-year colleges and universities, whereas new students plan to enter public community colleges or vocational schools" (1971, p. 15). In addition, we found the community college elite tended to be slightly older than the average community college student, and they did not seem to be happy with the state of their lives when they decided to enter a community college. They looked to college as a turning point, a means of changing their lives and finding better jobs.

Even students who are the children of professional and managerial families who apply to and eventually attend one of the most selective colleges and universities are often uninformed about the potential match between that institution's assets and liabilities and their own still unexplored potentialities and vulnerabilities. Those we term the community college elite have had even less information about the particular community colleges they entered and postsecondary education in general. Since colleges and universities had not been a part of their world of experience, they were confused by the terminology and jargon of higher education. They did not grasp the differences in faculty rank or in degrees, and they did not understand the specifics of the distinctions among colleges and universities; at most, they had a vague sense that "private" schools were supposed to be better than "state" schools. One woman, a resident of Boston for more than thirty-five years, when asked how her friends felt about her choice of a community college instead of a university, told us: "Most people I am around don't know the difference between community college and university. They just don't know about colleges. They don't even know what's in Boston. To them, a college is a college is a college."

A general lack of self-confidence in their ability to do college work was another common theme throughout the interviews with the community college elite. As already indicated, most of them had poor high school records; many had not graduated from high school; a few had already tried college and dropped out; others had not been students for several years. "I didn't think I would be able to make it," many students told us, and the depth of their self-doubt was reflected time and time again, as illustrated in the following excerpts from our interviews: "I was excited and scared about going there, [to the community college]. When I got there, there were people who had good educations in high school. They knew how to write and how to type, and I didn't know any of that. I didn't know where to turn."

"They let me pick a school. A counselor there advised me to look into [a local] community college because there, she told me, if you can do it, they keep you, and if you can't, they throw you out. I can remember liking that idea because I thought I would get thrown out and then the state would have to support me for the rest of my life. I never thought I could make it through two years of college." Naturally, this statement about liking the idea of being thrown out of college conceals despair by apparent defiance and cannot be taken at face value; nevertheless, the student just quoted is one of a larger and less ambivalent group we interviewed. Their lack of self-confidence was a principal reason for choosing a community college. "I went to [blank] community college to see if I could do it, school, that is. I was twenty-five, and that was part of the reason why I didn't go to Loyola. I didn't think I would be able to study. I didn't think I could cut it."

A good many of the community college elite chose community colleges for the same reasons other students did: very low tuitions, which can usually be covered in part by financial aid; except in rural areas, they are convenient—usually right in the neighborhood and accessible by public transport; their programs are sufficiently flexible to make it possible to hold part-time or even full-time jobs while attending; and the community colleges have a policy of open admissions to the institution as a whole (there are no requirements or entrance examinations to serve as hurdles—many of the students expressed surprise at how easy admission had been).

These students generally believe that they would not have been admitted to independent colleges or universities at the time they chose a community college. However, the drop in enrollments and the hunger for FTE in the public sector and its body-count equivalent in the private sector have meant that these colleges are not so difficult to get into as they appear; many of the community college students would in fact have been admitted had they applied. However, none of them even remotely considered an independent college or university. Similarly, these students took the stated tuition as the fixed price of the independent colleges and universities, not being aware that the fixed price is a sham: the top figure on a sliding scale which depends on the amount of financial aid the institution, in combination with the student, can make into a financial aid package. But again, what matters is perception, not reality, and what the students "knew" about the independent schools was that they were hard to get into and expensive — quite out of their reach. Since in high school they had not thought of themselves as college bound, they never made contact with a counselor or college recruiter who might have set them straight. Many harbored aspirations for college but thought these fanciful and did not have the expectation of ever reaching college.

First Semester — Psyching-Up

All of the students interviewed had a very positive experience in their first semester at their community colleges. Sometimes to their surprise, but always to their delight, they found that they not only could do college work, but could do it well — they all did above average work, and some got all As. Even the few who did not receive especially high marks their first semester experienced a tremendous boost in their self-confidence. As one woman, an immigrant and single parent with three children, explained: "My first semester I got one B and the rest Cs, and I felt good. I knew at least I didn't fail, and I knew I wasn't as bad as some others." A few said that they had found the school work easier than they had expected, but all of them took school obligations seriously; they completed their assignments on time, they studied regularly, and consequently, they did quite well.

At this early point in their college careers, anxious to assess their academic accomplishments and equipped with only limited knowledge of other colleges, the community college elite quite naturally turned to the other students in the college as a reference group with which to compare and evaluate themselves. Their community college was their "frog pond" (Davis, 1966; cf. Bassis, 1977), and in comparing themselves to the majority of their fellow students, they came off very favorably. Many of these students found for the first time that they were the "smart ones," and they liked the feeling. Two former high school dropouts described the effects of their initial success: "I felt great going to [blank] community college. I was number one in my accounting class, and I had a part-time job running the accounting lab for one year. I just couldn't believe I was making it."

"I had a 3.0 at [blank] community college. I did very well for me. I studied very hard. I was afraid I might fail, and I guess it became a good habit. I enjoyed doing well in school, and I felt really good about myself." Initial academic success served as an impetus for further involvement with the community college. Students who had begun on a part-time basis for fear of not being able to "hack it" or because of holding down part-time jobs enrolled as full-time students. To help support themselves, almost all of these students worked part-time at their community colleges, and, before long, they found that they were at the college every day for several hours, for both work and study. Not only were they studying and working at their community colleges, but increasingly the college environment became part of their social life. A number of the community college elite became involved in campus politics and student government. They were likely candidates because they were good students and already spent a good deal of time at the college.

Their academic achievement, although it won distinction, also brought the animosity of many fellow students. In the American grain, punishment of student "rate-busters" or DARs (Damned Average Raisers) has been endemic, perhaps especially among males. In his study of students at a community college London (1978) discovered in the general student culture powerful mores, almost amounting to sanctions, against academic achievement. The community college elite responded to these pressures with resentment and animosity vis-à-vis most of their fellow students, labeling them as lazy, immature, and "in it only for the money."

Because they shared common concerns and common enemies (due to the resentments they aroused), members of the community college elite, even in the fluid setting of a community college, recognized each other as potential allies. This was not inevitable; often in such situations individuals seek to avoid being identified with a group that is frowned upon; at any rate their ambivalence stirred from within by their resentment from without, led them to resist identification with those in the same academic boat. However, these individuals did not compete with each other, either for faculty favor or to avoid student disfavor, but instead formed small, supportive peer groups — encouraging and not belittling each other's academic efforts. At state universities and relatively unselective liberal arts colleges, there are institutional efforts to form such groups (as honors programs which have special facilities and special faculty attention), but in the instances we are describing, the noncompetitive groups were the creation of particular cadres of students, creating for themselves a substantial part of the social and academic environments.

A woman at a selective New England university described her community college support group as an important part of her community college experience: "There was a group of six of us in the corrections program. We all got along very well and would go over to each other's houses and study together and help each other. It was like if one person didn't understand something, one of the others would help them." Still stronger feelings were expressed by another woman student: "I loved my classmates. They were all great people. I have about six friends that I've stayed close to. I got more than an education at [blank] community college. Academically it was good, but I learned more about people there; the people were so warm and optimistic, and before going there, everyone I knew was pessimistic. I met a lot of people like myself, and that was very rewarding. I met people who were motivated to do something with themselves other than sit home and rot and become eggplants."

Important as these support groups were, there is a still more influential element accounting for their success: faculty interest and support. Just as the grades received in first-semester courses were a shorthand for faculty response, so an active faculty interest could legitimate the judgment that one might overcome initial handicaps and feelings of powerlessness.

Teachers in any institution are likely to take a personal interest in responsive and intelligent students, but this is especially true in community colleges where, as London has described them, most students are not responsive or interested in their courses or instructors. One former community college instructor explained: "When you stand up there in front of the class and look out into the sea of bored or distracted eyes and see one pair of bright eyes shining back at you, you naturally key in on them."

London interviewed a number of community college faculty, and he recorded one teacher's explanation for conferring special attention on these students. "I think the most satisfying kind of student for the community college teacher is the student who never intended to go to college, never felt he or she had the academic ability or never had the financial resources or whatever, came to the community college more or less because it was there, and found himself or herself, and found a field of study, be it career or transfer, and then went on and made a future from nothing. I've had students like that that found their opportunity, found themselves in the community college, and this is tremendously satisfying. One student like that can make up for a hundred of another kind, but it does not happen all that often that I know" (1978, p. 127).

The community college elite received special attention from at least one or two, and usually more, faculty members. We asked one student to describe her community college, and she began by describing her relationships with faculty: "It was very friendly and warm. You knew your professors really well, even outside school. We all had a good time. You would still have to perform well in school, but we were friends outside school." All of the elite had the highest regard for most of their community college faculty: "I thought 90 percent of them were great people, really dedicated to students and making you learn. I think they were aware you were a nontraditional student and helped you learn. And not just the faculty were great, also the secretaries, everyone there. I can't say I met one negative person at [blank] community college. I think one requirement in hiring people there was that they be a smiley person, optimistic and friendly, willing to help you in any way. I felt they really cared."

This aggregation of factors—initial academic success, increased involvement in the college environment, formation of a student support group, and special attention from respected faculty—provided the community college elite an impetus that countered their previous negative experiences with school and their corresponding self-deprecation. Their self-confidence grew, and, like other attitudes, began to have self-confirming effects. Not only were these students successful; they were recognized as such. Their achievements delighted them; the attitudes of faculty members heartened and even flattered them. We want to make clear that we are not here singing the praises of "positive reinforcement" as such: we do not believe that the common practice of school and college teachers to praise students and then expect, as a result, that they will do better work is correct. The reinforcement comes originally from the work itself, which in turn wins faculty response; otherwise, positive reinforcement is either empty ritual or it leads to self-deception and eventually cynicism about both self and others.

Obstacles—Cooling Down

The American school system, from kindergarten through post-baccalaureate study, has some of the elements of a roller coaster. One may rise in elementary school, only to be at the bottom of the heap in junior high or middle school, be at the top in ninth grade, and in the tenth grade, one may again be at the bottom. A high school valedictorian comes to a college full of valedictorians, and the roller coaster takes a steep dip. It would be a rare person for whom self-confidence was not influenced by the roller coaster. By the start of their second year in community college, the students encountered a formidable array of social and psychological barriers to their continued educational success, and their aroused self-confidence was significantly cooled down. One way to interpret the shift is to recognize that, on entering the second year (not an invariable date: the impact may occur earlier or later), some of the community college elite are compelled to recognize that the frog pond they are in is, in the eyes of many, a rather shallow and insignificant one.

As the community college students moved beyond their initial forays into the institution, their altered orbits brought them the widely prevailing signals that community colleges do not enjoy an especially good reputation for academic excellence. Inevitably they encountered the popular conception that community colleges are little more than "high schools with ashtrays." The very achievements of the community college elite in their initial programs helped evoke snide remarks from jealous classmates and resentful neighborhood peers. This was a way to discount the academic success of the achievers and to undercut their accomplishments on the ground that community colleges are so easy that anyone could not only get into them but stay in them. One student who encountered such assessments repeatedly, described their effect: "When I said I was going to [blank] community college, the reaction of most people was a simple 'Oh.' So I started feeling funny when people asked me where I went to school. People told me it was an easy school." Some elite became so self-conscious about attending a community college that they actually tried to conceal the fact or to avoid the topic of college when they met friends.

But even more challenging than the criticism from their peers was the disparagement from some of their own community college faculty. Most of the students we interviewed recounted how at least one faculty person had told them that the school they were in was not a "real college," and that, if they had plans to transfer, they had better get ready for "real college work."

We had an insufficient number of interviews with disparaging faculty to draw general conclusions either as to the distribution of such faculty, or as to the reasons for resorting to this behavior. It may be that some faculty feel professionally at a standstill. Frustrated and bitter, rather than waiting for someone else to undermine their professional status by making derogatory remarks about their place of employment, they engage in what might be called a preventive strike — making public their "failure" and discounting the quality of their students and the institution. Still other faculty, perhaps originally motivated by idealism, may be reacting out of anger at what they interpret as student apathy — *apathy* meaning generally not sharing the speaker's own preoccupations — and hence punishing students. Some critical faculty members, like those London describes as radicals of various political persuasions, may have believed they were performing a service to students by raising their social consciousness and debunking student aspirations for what seemed to the faculty like "dead-end jobs."

But whatever the faculty motivation, vindictive or altruistic, the predominant impact on students was immediate and disturbing; the predominant response, resentment. In some instances, students told us that they went to complain to the college administration about faculty, or that they confronted faculty when they criticized the community college. One student told us of the reaction of her class when an instructor told them that a community college was not a real college: "When he started telling us that stuff, we said, 'So make it real. We don't want it to be easy. We want a real college.'"

If, as we have suggested, community college faculty play an important role in bolstering the fragile self-confidence of students, then it seems safe to assume that faculty criticisms will also have a part in discouraging students. One student told us: "The way he kept saying, just wait until you transfer to [blank] university. It's not like here. You'll have to work there. It scared me. I didn't think I'd be able to make it at the university."

Since in this particular chapter we are concentrating on the students who successfully navigated transfer to the independent sector, we are not dealing with instances where faculty criticisms of this sort produced the very cooling out for which many of these same faculty would attack the community college system as a whole. One might instead say that for those who stood up against these criticisms, the latter were useful in replacing an earlier hopeful naiveté with increasing sophistication, especially as they began to look into the possibility of transfer. Despite all efforts of community college leadership and of many students of higher education to carve out independent but in no way inferior missions for these institutions, they have rarely overcome even in their own minds the fact that there is a hierarchy in American education, or rather several hierarchies with some degree of overlap in different parts of the country. These students were discovering that the community colleges are usually placed at the bottom, notably so in the Northeast, but also in some measure elsewhere (Cohen, 1977; see also Cohen, this volume).

A dramatic instance is the case of a student who had transferred from a bankrupt independent two-year junior college from which accreditation had been removed and explained: "All I knew was that it was private. So I figured it had to be better than a community college."

The combined impact of these impressions and realities may very well, to return to Clark's phrase, cool out large numbers of students (Clark, 1960; however, see Clark, this volume). Disillusioned and discouraged, they see little reason to continue in college. We found that, as the students' consciousness was raised, their spirits declined, and students evidenced the *Groucho Marx syndrome*. This is based on one of the comedian's most famous one-liners, "I wouldn't belong to a club that would have me as a member." We suggest that, instead of feeling pride in their community college accomplishments, students become embarrassed by the very fact of attendance at a community college. An active community college advocate described how it happened to her:

"I know that when I graduated, I graduated *cum laude*. I was so proud. I mean I never finished high school, but then people would say, oh, it's an A.A. Oh, it's from a community college. Then I felt like I wanted to hide it. I felt like they looked down on it."

Fortunately, our community college elite had experienced enough reinforcement and their sense of self-confidence was strong enough to sustain the combined forces of the cooling out phenomenon, but not without some loss of confidence. Their psyched-up egos had been drastically cooled down, but not quite extinguished.

Graduation, Application, and Admission

Most of the students we interviewed applied to four-year schools before they graduated; almost all of them graduated and received their associate's degree. The diploma and public recognition given them at graduation—most of these students graduated from their community colleges with honors—served as tangible evidence of their accomplishments. But by now these students had come to realize that an A.A. degree would not make that much difference in their lives. As one of these students said: "I looked in the paper every day, and I never saw any jobs for people with an associate's advertised. I knew I'd have to go on to get a bachelor's to be an accountant." Another transfer student explained how her degree aspirations were tempered by reality: "When I first came here [the United States], I was told that a high school diploma was very important, then I was told you need at least a two-year degree, and then I knew that I needed a four-year degree. I thought if I stop now, I will work in a daycare center or be a teacher's aide, and I could have done that without college."

So it was, then, for very compelling reasons that these students decided to transfer to four-year institutions. In most of the states where we interviewed students there were agreements guaranteeing community college graduates admission to a state university or college and, although the students usually applied to these schools for transfer, they also applied to selective independent colleges and universities. This raises two important questions: What makes them apply to independent colleges? And, more important, what makes them think that they may be admitted?

Part of the answer to the first question is obvious: they had learned which schools had the best reputations, and they wanted to go to the best school they could. (Contrary to what many might suppose, not all students want to go to the most selective institutions even if they can be sure of admission; they may not want to work that hard. The community college elite, as we have sought to make clear, are not indolent, let alone "collegiate," but are determined achievers.) Beyond wanting the best education they could get, they also wanted to find out just how good their community college education had been. The social stigma attached to community college had left its mark, and the students had nagging doubts regarding the validity of their first two years which for a time had been so important to them. They were searching for some external validation of their earlier achievements, and admission to a recognized selective college or university would provide precisely that information. Although they were encouraged to apply to independent colleges — and in many cases the encouragement from community college faculty, counselors, and administrators made the difference between applying and not applying — the underlying theme in our interviews was that they did not expect admission, and, in effect, in applying to the selective independent college, they believed they had everything to gain and very little to lose.

A community college graduate, who had applied to what many people consider the most selective college in the country, told us that in her admission interview she had been insulted: "The woman who interviewed me was an incredible snob. She talked to me as if I was an auto mechanic when she found out that I had gone to community college." We commented that it seemed to us that she was risking a lot of self-esteem in applying to such a selective place and asked her if she would not have felt terrible if she had been refused admission, but she insisted that she was not risking anything: "I just wanted to see if I could get in. I didn't really think I would." And another community college transfer who applied to a very selective institution commented similarly: "I applied to [blank] because someone said I should and it was near my home, but I wasn't admitted. It was like a fantasy to go there. The way I feel is, why not try for the highest, you have nothing to lose."

That these students did not expect actually to be admitted is further indicated by the fact that in addition to being very selective, the independent colleges and universities to which they applied were also very expensive — far too expensive for these students to afford without financial assistance. Yet, when asked, the students said they were not, at the time of their application, aware of the extent of financial aid available, nor did they expect to get it. They were, however, well aware of the general cost and high tuition required, but they were not considering finances when they applied — they were only seeing if they could be admitted. Statements like "First things first, I thought. I worked on getting accepted first, and then I worried about financial aid" and "I was worried about money, but I figured I would first try to get in and then worry about money" were typical. Another student, when asked directly how he had planned to meet financial obligations at the expensive independent college to which he transferred, responded bluntly: "I didn't. I just applied and thought I'd deal with money if I got in."

A few of the elite did tell us that they had vague plans to take out student loans if they were admitted, but it seems reasonable that, if they had really expected to be admitted, they would have been more concerned about financial aid.

The students in our study were unaware that, in the interest of promoting local attendance, a number of independent colleges and universities, including, for example, Harvard, M.I.T., and Tufts, have designated special funds specifically to help support local students with their financial needs. Once admitted, the awarding of scholarships and various other types of financial aid to the community college elite was, of course, a crucial factor in making their attendance possible. There is little doubt that, without financial aid, they could not have realized the opportunity admission provided for them.

Unexpected as it was, the notification of admission to the independent college or university was a tremendous thrill for the community college elite. It was an affirmation of the legitimacy of their community college education and became a source of prestige and renewed self-confidence. Elated by their admission, these same students who in the past had been hesitant to admit or mention their community college attendance, now told everyone where they were going to go to school, and the change they experienced in people's reactions was dramatic. Upon informing his formerly critical corner chums of his new college, one student remembered, "They were really surprised. One of them said, 'They are actually taking your credits there?' They couldn't believe it. Another one said, 'Man, you must have really been working hard.'"

The elite themselves saw their admission as an expression of confidence by the college or university, and in a sort of reverse of the Groucho Marx syndrome, students seemed to feel something to the effect: "If a club that I know is very selective selects me, then I must be good enough to be a member," or, as one student put it, "They admitted me; that must mean I can make it, right?"

Transfer Shock

Much has been written of transfer shock, the phenomenon in which students experience an immediate drop in grades upon transfer and, consequently, become discouraged and drop out (Hill, 1965; Nolan and Hall, 1978). It is suggested that this is especially true for community college transfer students; however, we did not find the effects of transfer shock to be especially severe on the community college elite. To be sure, most did experience a decline in their grade point average as compared to their previously high averages in community college, but, significantly, they were not discouraged and they did not drop out. For one thing, they had not expected to do as well as they had in the community college (although some did do just as well from the very start); for another thing, it seemed that their perspective on higher education had altered slightly, and they saw themselves after transfer in a different frog pond, where despite lower grades they still received average or above average marks.

Obviously, transfer shock is less likely to have a strong effect on a student who expects the new college to be harder than the former one. The community college elite were anything but overconfident their first semester after transfer. One transfer student who graduated with honors from a community college described her first semester at her new school: "I had it in my mind that I wouldn't do as well at the university as at the community college because the teachers and students and everyone was telling me it's going to be harder there, it's real college there. That first semester was really rough on me. My first semester at the university I got all Bs, but I felt like, and I thought, I was getting all Fs. It was such a shocking experience. I was really scared of the professors; they weren't as friendly as they were in the community college. I felt like I was killing myself to make grades; then I got this letter that said I was on the dean's list; I was really overwhelmed."

Another transfer student, who subsequently received his B.S. in accounting, described considerable apprehension over transfer:"I was afraid that [blank] university would be too tough for me. I know that [blank] university is no Harvard, but it also has a good reputation, and I didn't think I was the caliber of student to go there."

The community college elite were making comparisons between colleges now, not just between students. The fact that they perceived themselves to be at a more selective college than their community college seemed to mitigate the effects of the lower grades they received after transfer. We suggest that (as Bassis, 1977, has argued for freshmen at selective colleges) the community college elite saw themselves as having moved to a larger frog pond—one that included several colleges, not just one.

One student expressed his conception of an expanded frog pond quite clearly: "I got a C and three Bs, but I figure a B here is as good as an A at [blank] community college." Sometimes, students were given this across-college perspective by staff at their new university. One woman described her experience at her admissions interview: "They really questioned Cs, and they said a C from a community college is equal to an F at the university."

It is important to remember, however, that while the elite experienced lower grades their first semester after transfer, they achieved with only one exception at least average or above average marks. Had they failed, as some do, it is likely that they would have dropped out, or at least considered doing so, but the same may be said for the four-year students who, after two successful years, fail in their junior year.

Naturally, the community college elite compared themselves with their fellow students at their new college, and as when they compared themselves with their classmates in the community colleges, they found they did not do so badly; "My first semester was a nervous time. I had a higher idea of my peers' work. I thought they were all doing so well, then I got some good grades. I saw that my grades were even better than some of theirs. I got to know some of the people, and I felt better."

Another transfer student in her first semester at a large university had just received her first exam results when we interviewed her: "I was really scared, but I got an A. I was really thrilled. The group I studied with got scores in the 70s and got Cs, and they have been in the system longer than me. I was flying. I don't think my feet have touched the ground for four days. If I can do it there, I can do it other places. There are more kids here with better backgrounds than me, but there is also a large group here with mediocre backgrounds."

None of the students we interviewed indicated any feeling of being intellectually or socially inferior to their new peers. When they noted discrepancies between native students and themselves they attributed their lower grades to their having slightly less developed skill levels at the time of transfer, to not having an equal knowledge base in a specific content area, or to not being wise to the system at their new school — not yet knowing what exactly was expected of them or which courses or professors to select. Some cited family responsibilities as interfering with their study time. Many of the community college elite had to work in order to finance their continued education, and sometimes they resented their classmates who did not have to work and accused them of being immature and spoiled: "Here at [blank] university many students seem to have had everything handed to them on a gold platter. I've had to work to get where I am. I don't know how they came to be so spoiled. I feel like if I wasn't working I'd have all As in my courses, and some students here complain about homework, and I feel that they have no right to complain, they have so much time to study and all they do is play and complain about how much work they have to do."

We have found that for a variety of reasons (including innate intelligence, strong motivation, discipline and hard work, and an expanded conception of their college world), the community college elite manages to cope with transfer shock and with initial apprehension and lack of self-confidence. They survive the difficult first semester. Once past the first semester, research has shown that the grades of community college transfer students generally continue to rise until there is no significant difference between theirs and the grades of four-year students (Knoell and Medsker, 1965; Nickens, 1972; Nolan and Hall, 1978). They gain self-confidence with respect to both their ability to do college work and their ability to compete with their classmates on an equal basis.

Why Did They Succeed?

While the community college elite seems to gain in self-respect by comparing themselves to their classmates, there is also reason to believe that they profit from their classmates' impression of the community college student. As expected, we found that the community college transfer students at independent colleges and universities encountered the same criticism and condescension from some of their new peers and faculty that they had as community college students. But they also encountered students and faculty who not only encouraged them to achieve, but also expected high achievement from them specifically because they were transfers from a community college. In other words, the transfer students found some people assuming not that they were dumb because they were from community colleges, but quite the opposite: they must be quite smart because they were admitted from community colleges. One woman at a very selective independent school described this experience: "My TAs told me when I first came here that I must be brilliant to get in from a community college, and it worked like a grapevine—I was brilliant before I had to prove myself. It seemed like I got As in everything. Instructors knew about me before I even started a course. I would talk to them the first day, and they would say oh, you are the student from a community college."

Other transfer students told us that about half of the students and faculty they met were either critical or resentful of their having come from a community college; naturally these attitudes were distressing. But other students greeted transfer students as special just because they were from a community college and expected great things of them. One reason why many four-year students at selective institutions would automatically have high expectations is that the members of the community college elite were in fact able and unique individuals; we would suggest two other explanations beyond that.

In most private colleges and universities, unlike the University of California with its Master Plan or Florida with its two-tier system in upper-division institutions, community college transfers are as a group very small; hence, when the four-year students encounter them, they automatically assume that they must be special since there are so few of them.

The second proposed explanation is more complex. The very presence of community college transfer students on campus at independent colleges and universities challenges the perceptions held by four-year students of both community colleges and their own institutions. If they share, as many people do, the conventional conception of community colleges as second-class institutions, as something less than "real" colleges, and they see the transfer student as a product of that type of institution, then they must consider the implications for their own college and their personal self-image. In still another variation of the Groucho Marx syndrome, the four-year student who entered as a freshman may ask himself: "What am I doing in a club that accepts transfers from a community college?" If they answer that question by admitting that community college transfer students are just as good as they are, then they may in effect be saying that neither they nor their club—the expensive independent college or university—is special. More simply, they would be admitting that they are no more than equal to community college students, that the first two years of their college may be equaled by two years at a community college. Alternatively, the four-year students are left with only one choice: placing rank on the community college transfer student. In this way they protect their status as students at elite schools. This new variation of the Groucho Marx syndrome works something like this: "You were admitted to my club from a community college; therefore, you must be brilliant."

Similarly, some faculty at selective independent schools are faced with either admitting that their colleagues in the less distinguished community colleges are doing just as good a job of educating students for their first two years, or they may choose to view the community college transfer student as a unique product of an ordinary, even second-rate, institution.

Whatever the explanation, the effect is the same. The community college elite are exposed to a strong dose of positive reinforcement (in some cases, it might be an overdose, but we encountered no such instances) in the form of acceptance and a series of affirmative expectations for their academic performance. These expectations help support the self-confidence of the community college elite and serve as a balance against the negative and critical opinions of the less generous students and faculty. They may act as a self-fulfilling prophecy, with the community college elite internalizing these high expectations.

The power of this particular self-fulfilling prophecy is dependent on two important variables, the number of community college transfer students enrolled on a given campus and the degree of selectivity of the school. Accordingly, the self-fulfilling prophecy will be more in evidence at the most selective colleges and universities (with very small numbers of community college transfer students enrolled) and significantly less apparent at less selective institutions (to which many students from community colleges transfer.)

We have tried to show, as reflected by our interviews, that the academic success of the community college elite involves a complex interplay of social and psychological factors converging at critical points in the educational career. We would hesitate to identify any single variable as the primary cause, but the students themselves had little difficulty in selecting the crucial element—unanimously, they pointed to their community college experience as the key to their success: "My community college was where I learned how to get around in college, how to be in front of classes. I developed my confidence there." "My community college gave me a lot of confidence that I wouldn't have had otherwise. It gave me two years of positive reinforcement."

The recurrent theme in these comments is that a community college, more than anything else in their experience, provided students with the opportunity to gain self-confidence. Students also mentioned basic learning skills critical for success in college, but eventually all of them returned to the "feelings" community college gave them. As one student stated clearly: "You have to feel that you can do something when you start college, and community college gives you that feeling."

There is no denying that members of the community college elite are both unique and talented individuals, but to explain their apparent success at independent colleges and universities as merely the result of their innate talents is to discount the validity of their own perceptions and to be unfair to their respective community colleges.

References

Astin, A. W. *Preventing Students from Dropping Out.* San Francisco: Jossey-Bass, 1975.

Astin, A. W. *Four Critical Years: Effects of College on Beliefs, Attitudes, and Knowledge.* San Francisco: Jossey-Bass, 1977.

Bassis, M. S. "The Campus as a Frog Pond: A Theoretical and Empirical Reassessment." *American Journal of Sociology,* 1977, *82,* 1318–1326.

Clark, B. R. "The 'Cooling Out' Function in Higher Education." *American Journal of Sociology,* 1960, *65,* 569–576.

Cohen, A. M. "The Social Equalization Fantasy." *Community College Review,* 1977, *5* (2), 74–82.

Cohen, A. M. "Counting the Transfer Students," *ERIC Junior College Resource Review.* July, 1979. 6pp. (ED 172 864).

Cross, K. P. *Beyond the Open Door: New Students to Higher Education.* San Francisco: Jossey-Bass, 1971.

Davis, J. A. "The Campus as a Frog Pond: An Application of the Theory of Relative Deprivation to Career Decisions of College Men." *American Journal of Sociology,* 1966, *72,* 17–31.

Hill, J. "Transfer Shock: The Academic Performance of the Junior College Transfer." *Journal of Experimental Education,* 1965, *33,* 201–216.

Knoell, D., and Medsker, L. *From Junior to Senior College—A National Study of the Transfer Student.* Washington, D.C.: American Council on Education, 1965. 111pp. (ED 013 632).

London, H. B. *The Culture of a Community College.* New York: Praeger, 1978.

Nickens, J. "'Transfer Shock or Transfer Ecstasy.'" Paper presented at the annual meeting of the Ameriican Educational Research Association. Chicago, Ill., April, 1972. (ED 061 925).

Nolan, E. J., and Hall, D. L. "Academic Performance of the Community College Transfer Student: A Five-Year Follow-up Study." *Journal of College Student Personnel,* 1978, *19,* 543–548.

Riesman, D. "Community Colleges: Some Tentative Hypotheses." *Community Services Catalyst,* 1978, *8* (2), 1–5.

Sacks, H. S. "'Bloody Monday': The Crisis of the High School Senior," in H. S. Sacks and Associates, *Hurdles: The Admissions Dilemma in American Higher Education.* New York: Atheneum, 1978, pp. 10–47.

William Neumann is a research assistant to David Riesman.

David Riesman is a Henry Ford II Professor of Social Sciences at Harvard University.

Financing in community colleges is analyzed from an economic perspective, but the authors conclude that developing a set of educational priorities for the 1980s is the first step schools must take.

The Community College Mission and Patterns of Funding

David W. Breneman
Susan C. Nelson

Although community colleges have been one of the fastest growing sectors of U.S. higher education in recent years, limited academic attention has been focused on their financing. In the course of preparing a book on that subject for the Brookings Institution, we have tried to blend the economists' concerns for equity and efficiency with the operational problems and issues that confront practitioners and policy makers. This chapter begins with an explanation of the public finance approach that we take as economists. It then discusses some of the state and local issues that we encountered in our conversations with community college leaders and policy making officials around the country, first in general terms and then in the specific contexts of four of the states that we visited at some length: Florida, Illinois, Texas, and California. The chapter concludes with recommendations for community college leaders to consider.

Economic Analysis

One of the first steps in any analysis is the selection of criteria. As economists, we naturally turned to the standard theoretical tools that our profession uses to examine all kinds of public services: efficiency and equity. Whether the issue is national defense, highways, welfare, or education, economists use these two criteria to analyze the problem of allocating society's scarce resources between the public and private sectors, as well as within each sector. The study for Brookings takes an economic perspective and hence examines the implications of efficiency and equity for the financing of community colleges.

When applied to publicly provided activities like education, the concept of efficiency offers guidance in determining *what* should be subsidized, while the notion of equity refers to *who* should be subsidized. To economists, efficiency means more than just producing something for the lowest cost. An efficient allocation of resources is said to occur if the benefits (both public and private) from the production of some good or service exceed by as much as possible the total costs (both public and private) of producing it. With most goods and services in society, an efficient level of production and consumption can be achieved through the operation of the free (nonsubsidized) market, since decisions of individual producers and consumers will take into account virtually all the costs and benefits involved. For activities that produce public as well as private benefits, however, individuals facing a full-cost price will demand too little (from society's perspective) of the good or service. Consequently, an efficient allocation of resources may require subsidies to encourage people to increase their consumption of activities like education. The amount of subsidy should not necessarily equal the total value of the public benefits but should just be sufficient to induce a socially optimal level of education.

Applying efficiency considerations to the financing of community colleges suggests that a balance between public and private sources of support seems justified. Starting with the presumption that attending a community college does yield private benefits, it is rational for students, or families, to be willing to pay some tuition. At the same time, since most people agree that there are also public benefits — for example, to the state and local community in having a more educated and trained labor force that increases its attractiveness to business and industry — efficiency also provides a rationale for subsidies from both state and local governments. The diversity of services offered by community colleges, however, leads to different mixes of public and private support. On one hand, activities where the benefits are essentially private should be financed primarily on a pay-as-you-go basis. On efficiency grounds, at least, there is little public interest served by encouraging additional participation in avocational courses such as poodle grooming and macramé. On the other hand, the substantial public benefits from encouraging adults who cannot read or write to take remedial courses argue for complete subsidy, and efficiency considerations suggest that little or no tuition be charged for these activities.

Efficiency is not the only criterion for judging a finance system; equity must also be taken into account. Equity is a more subjective concept than efficiency, so not surprisingly it has been interpreted in a number of ways by economists. Generally, though, it reflects a concern with the distribution of income in society and a concern that poor people have an opportunity for success. Since education is an important component of that opportunity, equity considerations are reflected in the concern that financial barriers not prevent low-income people from furthering their education.

At the community college level, two types of equity issues have emerged. First, there is broad agreement that some students deserve extra subsidy beyond that suggested by efficiency concerns. Whether this assistance should be provided by lowering tuition selectively with need-based aid or by universally setting it below the level consistent with efficiency remains the subject of heated debate. Second, in states with local support for community colleges, equity concerns are also voiced for residents of poor districts in a fashion similar to the school finance litigation that began in California with the Serrano case. Because of variations in district wealth, some communities can support their community colleges more generously and with lower tax rates than can other districts. Although this equity issue is less compelling for a number of reasons at the community college level than at the elementary/secondary level (foremost among them that attending a community college is not required, universal, a necessary right of citizenship), it is one among several considerations that state finance formulas should take into account in distributing state funds to local districts.

Combining the analyses of efficiency and equity suggests that the burden for financing community colleges should be shared by state government, local governments, and the students but that some groups might need additional subsidies. Tuition for students who are not disadvantaged should be set at whatever level is dictated by efficiency concerns, as far below cost as required by the presence of public benefits. Then equity for the disadvantaged could be accomplished by a selective lowering of tuition through student aid. After nearly a decade's experience with large-scale government programs of need-based student aid, the practical arguments against relying on student aid to achieve equity are substantially reduced, particularly if need-based student aid were combined with tuition waivers for special groups like the elderly and the educationally disadvantaged.

The key tuition issue boils down to a political evaluation of the public benefits of what community colleges are doing—of the benefits to society that students will not take into account in deciding whether to enroll. The issue in allocating this subsidy burden between state and local governments depends primarily on the distribution of these benefits between the state and the locality.

The principles of equity and efficiency cannot take us any farther in recommending how community colleges should be financed. Ultimately, the remaining questions are political and philosophical. Consequently, no single best finance formula emerges from our analysis.

This discussion of equity and efficiency does help to focus on the real sources of disagreements over finance. For instance, tension between mission and finance essentially arises from differing opinions on these efficiency and equity issues, on public benefits, and on who merits extra subsidy. Also, it is not sufficient to argue that community colleges could put $1 million in additional spending to good use in ways that would serve the public. It is necessary to argue that the state or local community would be better off if that $1 million were spent on community colleges than if it were left in the taxpayer's pocket, or if it were spent on other public services like highways or on other educational institutions. The future of community colleges will depend, in part, on how persuasively that case is made to the public.

State and Local Issues

On the basis of site visits to several states and discussions with numerous community college leaders and state and local officials, two general conclusions stand out. First, disputes over financing formulas often disguise fundamental disagreements over purpose, mission, and priorities. Much of the criticism of formulas is misdirected, therefore, because the problems are not technical, but substantive. Second, for practical reasons as well as the theoretical ones noted above, no "single best plan" for financing community colleges exists, and we do not propose one. The unique history and the different functions served by community colleges in the various states militate against a single method of finance being ideal in all cases. The criteria of equity and efficiency, combined with practical operating considerations, do provide guidance, however, in judging some approaches as clearly better than others, and these will be noted briefly.

Policy makers in each state that we visited were embroiled in highly specific debates over financing policy of little relevance elsewhere; nonetheless, several common themes, or issues, emerged from the visits. These common concerns included:

1. Aggregate levels of support, and the concern that budgets are not keeping pace with inflation and rising enrollments;
2. The balance between state and local support (in states with a local contribution), and how responsibilities should be divided;
3. Equalization of resources among districts with different property wealth (in states with local support);

4. Tuition levels, including what share of costs should be covered by tuition, and the relation to tuition charges in four-year public institutions within the state;

5. Financial support (or lack thereof) for community services and other noncredit activities;

6. Problems surrounding the distribution of state support, including the choice of formula (e.g., cost based vs. flat rate), the use of enrollment-driven formulas at a time of slow (or no) growth, and the lack of start-up funds for new programs.

In responding to issues such as these, the states exhibit a bewildering variety of formulas and budgetary procedures impossible to summarize briefly. Although various taxonomies have been proposed to categorize state plans, we have found it useful to consider finance plans as embodying a set of responses to choices that must be made in supporting a community college system. The basic choices that face state and local policy makers in developing a finance plan are: (1) Should the plan be simple or complex? (2) Should it involve public funding from the state only or should there be state and local sharing? (3) If there is sharing, should the state ignore, or attempt to offset, differences in revenue-raising among local jurisdictions? (4) Should program cost differences be considered or ignored? (5) Should tuition cover a specific portion of costs, or should colleges have discretion in setting it? (6) Should only courses for credit be financed or should support be provided for some — or all — noncredit courses? (7) Should the level of state support be linked to that provided to other public sectors of education, or should community colleges be treated in isolation? (8) Should the formula emphasize incentives for low-cost provision of services or simply reimburse colleges for the actual costs incurred? (In addition, there are several administrative and technical choices that influence the allocation of funds. Should there be strict line-item control or local discretion to shift funds among classes of expenditure? Should average costs or some form of incremental costs be used? Should cost parameters be based on systemwide averages (or medians) or should standard costs be used? Should differences in college size (and hence in unit costs) be considered or ignored? Should the formula be based on average daily attendance, weekly contact hours, or student credit hours?)

A state's financing plan can be described rather completely through the answers to these questions, which cover the principal policy decisions that must be made. Analysis and evaluation of a given state plan should focus on the implications of the set of choices embodied in the plan. Examples drawn from four of our state visits illustrate the types of choices made and some of their implications.

Florida. This state's system of community colleges is noteworthy on at least two counts: its strong tradition of local control despite the absence of local financial support and the use of a highly complex system of cost analysis for determining budgets. On the first point, it is commonly asserted that local control requires local financial support, but Florida is an exception to this rule. Local boards, appointed by the governor, exercise considerable policy control over the colleges, and administrators have wide-ranging discretion over the allocation of the budget. It is unclear how secure local control really is should the colleges fall into disfavor with the legislature; nonetheless, Florida currently stands as proof that significant local control is possible in a system that is publicly financed almost exclusively by state government.

The budget for Florida's community colleges is based upon detailed data on program costs in thirty-four fields of study, one of the most elaborate types of such financing currently in use in any community college system. An extensive data base is required for such a system, but states considering a move to cost-based funding should be aware that the level of detail required can be considerably less than that used in Florida. At issue is the trade-off between simplicity and complexity, and a case can be made for limiting the number of cost categories to five or six as a reasonable compromise.

A serious problem experienced in Florida has been the tendency to underestimate enrollments, with the result that unit costs are driven down artificially. These lower costs are then rebuilt into the next year's budget, forcing increased use of part-time faculty and other cost-saving efforts. Now that growth has slowed, it should be possible — and sensisible — to shift to prior year enrollments as the budget base rather than to attempt to forecast enrollments.

Texas. This state starkly poses the conflict of values between local decision making and equal educational opportunities regardless of residence. Local communities must vote to create a community college district and are responsible for physical plant construction and maintenance; the state pays for instructional costs, making no distinction in its payments between rich and poor districts. The result is wide disparity in facilities and resources among community college districts in Texas. Dallas and Ft. Worth, for example, strongly support their colleges, providing superb facilities and substantial local tax revenues, while Austin and Houston have not yet voted to authorize a local tax in their districts. Austin Community College has no permanent campus, operating instead out of rented space in downtown Austin and out of buildings converted from other uses. A further difficulty in Texas is that many of the older campuses serve an area much larger than the district's tax base and have not been successful in expanding that base. Because the state makes no attempt to equalize resources among districts, the extremes in resources are probably as great in Texas as anywhere in the country. A state policy that ignores these differences in district resources is hard to justify, unless overarching value is placed on the college as a purely local institution.

Illinois. Although we do not advance a model finance formula, the approach followed in Illinois comes closer to an ideal meeting our criteria—efficiency and equity—than any other state we visited. The state uses a complex formula that incorporates inflation factors, growth factors, program cost differences, an equalization provision recognizing differences in district wealth, and categorical grants for disadvantaged students. Local boards retain important authority, including the power to set tuition. Program costs are collected in five categories—Baccalaureate (college transfer), Business Occupational, Technical Occupational, Health Occupational, and General Studies—and state payments are based on systemwide average costs in each category. This technique rewards efficient operation, yielding a surplus for campuses that keep costs below the average. In a recent change, future budgets will be based on the most recent year's actual enrollments, rather than on forecast levels.

The principal problems under this plan occur because the Chicago district is so much larger than the others. In certain areas, such as General Studies, Chicago produces a large proportion of total instruction in the state, and its costs tend to dominate the systemwide average cost of instruction. The result is a lower state payment than would otherwise exist, hurting smaller campuses that cannot achieve Chicago's economies of scale. One drawback of a plan that operates on systemwide averages is that sharp differences in size and costs will generate inequities among campuses. Consequently, one can foresee a continuing need in Illinois for periodic adjustments to the formula.

California. By far the largest community college state, California has tended to finance its two-year colleges more like elementary/secondary schools than like a part of higher education. The commitment to no tuition reflects this orientation, and California is the only state with such a policy. In our view, many community college leaders in California exaggerate the importance of tuition-free status, ignoring both the experience of other states and the phenomenal growth of federal and state student aid programs. In fact, prior to the passage of Proposition 13, virtually all two-year college activities were fully subsidized, whether for credit, noncredit, or community service. We suspect that these extraordinarily generous subsidies contributed in a small way to the taxpayer revolt in which California leads the nation.

Since passage of Proposition 13, financing of community colleges, as with other social services, has been conducted under near-crisis conditions. The one-year bailout bill replaced with state dollars much of the local revenue that was lost, in a fashion that continued expenditure differences based on district wealth. The new finance plan, A.B.8, does little better, leaving the state in the dubious position of perpetuating differences in local wealth. Attempts at equalization proved politically impossible at a time when total revenues were being cut, and there is a strong possibility that a Serrano-type lawsuit will be filed against the system. Whether the courts will extend the precedent of school finance reform to community colleges is an open — and inter-esting — question.

Had Proposition 9 passed in June 1980, the required cut in state income taxes coupled with the continuing impact of Proposition 13 would have forced the rise of tuition in all public institutions of higher education in the state, including community colleges. Although Proposition 9 was defeated, the possibility of tuition being required for community colleges in the 1980s remains strong and to resist stubbornly and refuse to plan for it seems to us a self-defeating approach.

The Future

Tension between mission and finance promises to become more pressing in the 1980s as resources for higher education become less plentiful. Institutional leaders will be forced to choose which activities are central to the college and which are of lesser importance. Perhaps the most fundamental choice facing community colleges is whether to emphasize the community-based learning center concept, with an emphasis on adult and continuing education and community services, or to emphasize transfer programs, sacrificing elsewhere if necessary. During the years of greatest growth, such choices were avoided by adhering to the model of a comprehensive community college striving to meet every possible need. Shrinking resources may force the choice between remaining a part of traditional higher education or moving to become a community-based service organization. It may no longer be possible to have it both ways.

We conclude with some brief recommendations for community college leaders to consider. First, as noted above, there is a need to set priorities among activities, deciding which are critical to the institu-tion. We did not come away from our state visits with the sense that many colleges had developed a set of priorities for the 1980s, although it seems certain that budgets will be tight. Similarly, there needs to be greater recognition that just because an activity has value is not a suffi-cient argument for public subsidy. Arguments for support must become more sophisticated and discerning.

Second, too much emphasis is placed on maximizing enroll-ments, without reference to educational value. Budget formulas during the 1960s and '70s may have placed a premium on enrollment growth, but enrollment-driven formulas are likely to be deemphasized in the

1980s. Instead, an ability to explain who benefits—and in what way—from enrolling in various courses and programs may be of increased importance. Hence, better assessment techniques must be developed if the case for increased public subsidy is to be made convincingly.

Third, cost comparisons with other public institutions are likely to be misleading and should be avoided. Universities and community colleges are complex institutions, and computations of average cost per FTE student are not very reliable for guiding state resource allocation. The cost structure within community colleges is certainly worth further investigation when focused on comparisons among two-year institutions.

Fourth, we suspect that community service activities will remain largely on a pay-as-you-go basis; rather than bemoan that prospect, efforts should be concentrated on ways to operate with limited subsidies. Alternatively, it would be perfectly reasonable for a college not to stress activities supported primarily from student fees.

Fifth, discretion is essential in selecting courses in the community service area, even if no public funds are involved. In virtually every state we visited, controversy was raging over some course being offered by the community college—macramé, belly dancing, cake decorating, poodle grooming, to name but a few. The damage to public relations must be weighed against the value of offering such courses.

Our final observation is that community college leaders in the 1980s must recognize limits, resisting the temptation to spread resources so thinly that quality is lost. This decade provides an opportunity to consolidate gains from the era of rapid growth. As the mission of community colleges becomes more focused and as priorities are determined, it should be possible to reduce tension between mission and finance that we encountered in the states studied. Failing that clarification, the financing of community colleges will become increasingly controversial in the difficult years ahead.

David W. Breneman is senior fellow and Susan Nelson is
research associate at the Brookings Institution in
Washington, D.C.

A statistical breakdown of background of community
college students reveals less curriculum tracking than
generally maintained. However, the increasing diversity
of students enrolled in technical programs may
complicate class-based tracking.

Curriculum Tracking and Social Inequality in the Community College

Robert G. Templin, Jr.
Ronald W. Shearon

One of the most critical attacks upon the two-year college to emerge during the 1970s revolves around the relationship of the community college with the American social class structure. One part of the assault charges that the two-year institution offers little real opportunity for upward social mobility because the American system of higher education itself is stratified. Since the two-year college is at the bottom of this hierarchy, community college students are destined to remain at the lower levels of the social class structure as well (Karabel, 1972; Zwerling, 1976). A second and more direct attack alleges that community colleges tend to perpetuate the existing class structure by tracking students into programs that lead to jobs which are roughly commensurate with the students' present socioeconomic status (Zwerling and Park, 1974).

Defenders of the community college argue that such attacks are unwarranted. Some maintain that the open-door policy represents a direct challenge to the kinds of elitist values once held in American higher education (Monroe, 1972). Others argue that the creation of the community college began an important democratizing movement providing access and educational opportunity, which has resulted in upward social mobility for the poor and disadvantaged (Gleazer, 1980).

Context of the Debate

Actually, both the criticism and defense of the community college described above are reflective of a much wider debate among sociologists over the nature of the American class structure itself. Both educators and sociologists have long recognized the importance of the relationship between the education one receives and the socioeconomic status ultimately attained. However, there is sharp disagreement between sociological theorists and researchers over whether the class structure itself is actually necessary, what the underlying factors are that determine the type and amount of education a person receives, and the ultimate effects of education on social mobility (Karabel and Halsey, 1977).

According to functional theorists in sociology (Davis and Moore, 1966), social stratification is both necessary and positive due to the requirement that society must have some means to motivate and assure that individuals are distributed among the different positions which make up that society's division of labor. Especially in a technological society where some positions require more skill and training or are more difficult to perform than others, society by necessity must provide some mechanism to ensure that important and difficult positions are filled by persons with the greatest talent. To motivate able persons to fill critical positions, society must employ a mechanism of unequal rewards. Thus, structured inequality or social stratification is created and maintained by society.

Carrying the functionalist argument further, functional theories of education maintain that in the American class structure, higher education serves as the means for the selection, training, and placement of individuals in positions commensurate with their abilities. The community college in particular is viewed as being well suited to serve as a channel for social mobility and for the attainment of the American ideal of achieving social position based upon motivation, ability, and performance rather than of the basis of race, sex, or family origin. Clark (1962, p. 3) assumes this position arguing, "Our age demands army upon army of skilled technicians and professional experts, and to the task of preparing these men the educational system is increasingly dedicated." However, to meet this societal need higher education must assume a sorting function based upon a person's ability. "Democracy encourages aspiration, and generous admission allows the student to carry his hopes into the school or now principally the college. But there his desires run into the standards necessary for the integrity of programs and the training of competent workers. The college offers the opportunity to try, but the student's own ability and his accumulative record of performance finally insist that he be sorted out" (Clark, 1962, p. 80).

Functional theories of social stratification and education build a basis upon which supporters can claim the two-year college functions to assure equal opportunity as well as a mechanism to assure that societal needs are met.

Presenting an opposite stand is a sociological perspective known as the conflict theory of social stratification. This viewpoint maintains that social stratification is neither necessary nor serves to guarantee the most able persons will fill the most important positions in society. Rather, the class structure serves those who are powerful and wealthy by institutionalizing their privileges and enabling them to pass their social status on to their children. Such a system results in the maintenance of the status quo and the perpetuation of social inequality based upon socioeconomic privilege (Dahrendorf, 1959; Lenski, 1966).

Authors applying the conflict theory to education maintain that while there is a relationship between the education a person receives and the eventual position attained in the social hierarchy, educational opportunities are not equal but are based upon the class privileges of the student's family (Collins, 1971). The implications of this position are that students receive educations roughly corresponding to their parents' position in society, regardless of their abilities, motivations, or performance. As such, higher education, especially the community college, acts to justify and perpetuate the existing stratification system in the United States by distributing educational opportunities and resources unequally and according to individual socioeconomic status. Comprehensiveness is merely a guise under which the two-year colleges track students from lower socioeconomic backgrounds into occupational programs while those from more affluent family origins are admitted to college transfer curricula. One proponent of this view (Karabel, 1972, p. 551) writes: "In a stratified society, what this diversity of educational experiences is likely to mean is that people will, at best, have an equal opportunity to obtain an education that will fit them into their appropriate position in the class structure. More often than not, those of lower-class origins will under the new definition of equality of educational opportunity, find themselves in schools or curricula which will train them for positions roughly commensurate with their social origins."

The community college with its open-door philosophy and comprehensive curricula are held to be merely symbolic gestures to equal opportunity. As other writers (Zwerling and Park, 1974) point out, the community college merely presents the illusion of opportunity to those from lower-socioeconomic-status backgrounds who are ultimately either flunked out of college transfer programs or tracked into occupational programs.

Research on Tracking

Two studies on community college students were conducted in an attempt to establish empirically whether either the functionalist or conflict theories of social stratification and education actually describe program activity of community colleges. The first study was initiated in 1974 using a sample of 6,937 curriculum students enrolled in sixteen, two-year institutions in the North Carolina Community College System (Shearon, Templin, Daniel, 1976). The second research effort was conducted in 1979 with a sample of 11,888 curriculum students enrolled in fifty-seven North Carolina community colleges and technical institutes (Shearon and others, 1980). In both studies information regarding student socioeconomic status, academic ability, curriculum, and demographic characteristics was collected and analyzed. One of the issues addressed was the extent to which, if any, community colleges are systematically tracking students into programs according to their socioeconomic status.

Results from both studies generally confirmed that students' socioeconomic status characteristics were associated with the curriculum in which students eventually enrolled. There indeed appears to be some merit to Zwerling's charges that community college programs are stratified in a relationship which roughly mirrors the socioeconomic status of students. However, there also appears to be a relationship between academic ability and program selection which is independent of socioeconomic status just as functionalist theorists such as Clark might predict.

As demonstrated in Table 1, the 1979 study showed transfer students are more likely to come from families with upper incomes, with parents who are well educated and whose head-of-household is a professional or white-collar worker than are students enrolled in either technical or vocational programs. Vocational students especially are more likely to reflect the expected sorts of opposite characteristics. Vocational students are more likely not to have graduated from high school and are nearly three times more likely to be nonwhite than are transfer students. When results of the two studies were compared over the five years separating them, the findings were remarkably consistent.

In addition to the above, each of the studies employed stepwise multiple regression analyses to study the extent to which student socio-

Table 1. Percentage Distribution of Curriculum Students
Enrolled in the North Carolina Community College System, 1979
by Selected Demographic, Socioeconomic, and Ability Characteristics
(n = 11,888)

Variable		Curriculum		
		College Transfer	Technical	Vocational
Race:				
White		83	74	69
Non-White		17	26	31
	Total	100	100	100
Family Income:				
Less than $10,000		42	45	51
$10,000–19,999		28	35	36
$20,000 or more		30	20	13
	Total	100	100	100
Occupation of Head of Household:				
White Collar		58	43	27
Blue Collar		25	35	49
Unskilled and Farm		17	22	24
	Total	100	100	100
Father's Education:				
Less than High School Graduate		37	49	59
High School Graduate or Equivalent		30	29	26
Some College		14	10	7
College Graduate or More		19	12	8
	Total	100	100	100
High School Rank:				
Upper One Third		36	32	20
Middle One Third		53	53	51
Lower One Third		5	6	8
Did not Graduate from High School		6	9	21
	Total	100	100	100

economic status and ability characteristics were good predictors of the
type of program a student would enter. Using this approach, student
socioeconomic, academic, and demographic characteristics were taken
into account statistically so that interactions between these variables
and their relationship with curriculum enrollment could be studied.
When these variables were all taken into account simultaneously and

the independent relationship of each with educational program selected was studied, the results described a somewhat different picture than that portrayed in Table 1.

Although a positive relationship was detected between students' socioeconomic status characteristics and the educational program in which they enrolled, this relationship was neither consistent across all socioeconomic variables, nor was it a particularly strong relationship. For example, the higher the students' educational level, family income, and the parents' educational level, the more likely were those students to be enrolled in college transfer programs. Conversely, the lower the students' levels with respect to those characteristics, the more likely they were to be enrolled in vocational programs. However, no such relationship was observed with respect to the occupational status of the head-of-household. In addition, whereas a positive relationship was observed between socioeconomic status and educational program area selection, the relationship was consistently weak, as measured by a variety of statistical correlation tests. Given these limiting conditions, while the research findings conclusively demonstrated a relationship between socioeconomic status characteristics and program enrollment, it is equally clear that such a weak relationship makes it unlikely that community colleges are systematically tracking their lower-socioeconomic students into technical and vocational programs.

Consequently, those who charge the community college with tracking students according to their social origin raise a valid issue which should not be ignored. However, the problem of tracking can be easily overplayed with the inference that it is a pervasive activity in the two-year college which seriously threatens equal educational opportunity. The findings of the research reported in this article simply do not support such a conclusion.

Changing Enrollments in Technical Programs

One of the major factors identified by Zwerling (1976) as contributing to the community college's role in perpetuating social inequality is its creation of occupational programs into which lower-socioeconomic-status students are tracked. From his writings he describes curriculum comprehensiveness as being in reality a hierarchy of programs in which transfer programs are at the top of the pyramid with occupational programs at the bottom. An additional characteristic which he ascribes to career programs are that they tend to be dead-end or terminal curricula which do not contribute to students' upward social mobility.

Results from the two North Carolina studies raise some challenges to Zwerling's description of occupational programs, especially those in the technologies, and their relationship to upward social mobility. One of the trends observed in both studies of North Carolina community college students enrolling in technical programs was the increasing diversity of student characteristics. In particular, it was found that not only have enrollments grown disproportionately faster in the technologies than in college transfer programs, but students in technical programs increasingly represented upper-income and occupational groups.

Results also revealed that greater numbers of students who previously attended four-year colleges and universities full time are deciding to turn to community colleges and to programs in the technologies in particular. For example, 15 percent of technical students in 1974 had been enrolled full time at a four-year college or university prior to their community college enrollment. Five years later the percentage had grown so that nearly 20 percent of all students enrolled for technical degrees had earlier been full-time four-year college or university students. In 1979, 6 percent of all students pursuing an associate's degree in the technologies already had an earned baccalaureate. These students do not at all resemble the working class poor which Zwerling attributes to occupational programs. On the contrary, an increasing proportion of students enrolling in technical programs not only come from relatively affluent backgrounds, but in many respects they actually equal or exceed the socioeconomic status characteristics of the typical college transfer student.

While the data will not support definitive statements on the matter, they do suggest a number of possibilities and lead to some speculation regarding student socioeconomic status and changing enrollments in technical programs. First, it is possible that a hierarchy of programs related to student socioeconomic status does exist but that certain programs in the technologies are no longer second to transfer programs in the educational hierarchy. Second, certain programs in the high technologies such as those in health, engineering, and computer-related fields may now be emerging to share the upper reaches of the pyramid with certain college transfer programs. Perhaps more important than the traditional hierarchy of programs between college transfer and technical programs, could be the development of a hierarchy among programs in the technologies themselves.

As for Zwerling's assumption that occupational curriculums are terminal programs which do not promote social mobility, the 1979 study of community college students found that 41 percent of students enrolled in technical programs actually planned to transfer to a four-year college to earn their baccalaureate. Other recent evidence (Kintzer, 1980) indicates that articulation efforts between two- and four-year colleges toward the development of "2 plus 2" agreements in the technologies are expanding.

Occupational programs in technical fields are now expected by students to give them both a marketable skill and the opportunity to transfer to a four-year college or university. Thus while some of Zwerling's observations may remain valid for many vocational and lower-level paraprofessional programs, the generalization no longer convincingly applies to technical curricula. For instance, high school graduation, grade point averages, or standardized test scores may not be valid predictors of ability for mature adults who are highly motivated. Denial of admission to a technical program because it is filled with students who previously attended four-year colleges and have already earned their baccalaureate does not mean students denied admission are unable to succeed. It does mean that such conditions will make program admission in certain technologies increasingly difficult for those who traditionally looked to the community college for opportunities of upward social mobility. Institutions which deny admission to programs on the basis of the foregoing criteria in effect could be reenforcing class-based curriculum tracking since those who are most likely to lack the proper credentials are also those most likely to be from lower socioeconomic backgrounds.

There are a number of steps which community colleges are taking or can take to minimize the prospects of any latent institutional practice of tracking by student socioeconomic status. (1) Program admission policies can be reevaluated both in transfer and technical programs to assure that criteria are valid and related to skills necessary to complete the program. (2) Program admissions policies can be structured so that a commitment to a minimum number of high-risk or non-traditional students is made. (3) Counseling programs are now being designed to help students make educational program choices and career decisions based on more complete information and on a more rational basis. (4) Outreach efforts, not just on an institutional basis but on a program basis as well, can be made to encourage more than a simple passive accessibility to programs by students from lower socioeconomic backgrounds. (5) Curricula are being designed so that vocational programs apply in great part toward a technical degree in the same field. Programs in the technologies also can be constructed so as to maintain the transfer option toward the baccalaureate.

The remedy to the problem of inequality of opportunity for the poor will not be found in altering the educational system alone without making corresponding changes in other sectors of society. But recognizing the extent to which program hierarchies and socioeconomic tracking may exist and minimizing their negative effects are first steps in reducing inequalities of educational opportunity in the community college.

References

Clark, B. R. *Educating the Expert Society.* San Francisco: Chandler, 1962.
Collins, R. "Functional and Conflict Theories of Educational Stratification." *American Sociological Review,* 1971, *36* (6), 1002–1019.
Dahrendorf, R. *Class and Class Conflict in Industrial Society.* Stanford: Stanford University Press, 1959.
Davis, K., and Moore, W. E. "Some Principles of Stratification." In R. Bendix and S. W. Lipset (Eds.), *Class, Status, and Power.* New York: The Free Press, 1966.
Gleazer, E. J. *The Community College: Values, Vision, and Vitality.* Washington, D.C.: American Association of Community and Junior Colleges, 1980.
Karabel, J. "Community Colleges and Social Stratification." *Harvard Educational Review,* 1972, *42,* 521–562.
Karabel, J., and Halsey, A. H. (Eds.). *Power and Ideology in Education.* New York: Oxford University Press, 1977.
Kintzer, F. C. "Articulation/Transfer: Vocational Technical and Occupational Education." *OEC Newsletter,* 1980, *56,* 8–12.
Lenski, G. *Power and Privilege: A Theory of Social Stratification.* New York: McGraw-Hill, 1966.
Monroe, C. R. *Profile of the Community College: A Handbook.* San Francisco: Jossey-Bass, 1972.
Shearon, R., and others. *Profile of Students in North Carolina Community Colleges and Technical Institutes. Volume I — Technical Report [and] A Summary of Research Findings.* Raleigh: North Carolina State Univ., Dept. of Adult and Community College Education, 1976. 379pp. ED 136 846.
Shearon, R., and others. "1979 Profile of North Carolina Community College and Technical Institute Students: A Preliminary Summary of Findings." Paper presented to the American Educational Research Association Special Interest Group for Community Junior College Research, Boston, April 7, 1980. 16pp. ED 184 643.
Zwerling, L. S. *Second Best: The Crisis of the Community College.* New York: McGraw-Hill, 1976.
Zwerling, L. S. and Park, D., Jr., "Curriculum Comprehensiveness and Tracking: The Community College's Commitment to Failure." *Community College Review,* 1974, *2,* 10–20.

Robert C. Templin, Jr., is dean of instruction at Piedmont Virginia Community College and center associate, Center for the Study of Higher Education, University of Virginia, Charlottesville.

Ronald W. Shearon is professor of adult and community college education, North Carolina State University, Raleigh.

If community colleges are going to educate—
rather than exploit—new "new" students, their real
needs and aspirations must be identified.

The New "New Student": The Working Adult

L. Steven Zwerling

During the 1960s and into the early '70s, a new two-year college opened virtually every week. Enrollments seemed to increase exponentially, with no apparent limit in sight. In 1978, however, for the first time in twenty years there was a 1 percent drop in total community college enrollment.

These gross figures mask another phenomenon—the growth in the number of adult part-time students. Actually, since the early 1970s there have been more part-time students attending two-year colleges than traditional, full-time eighteen- to twenty-one-year-olds. There is general agreement that the gap in numbers between part- and full-time students will continue to widen during the 1980s though there is controversy regarding specifics.

The National Center for Education Statistics projects a more than 50 percent rise in community college enrollments between 1976 and 1986—with adult part-time students accounting for most of the increase (Scully, 1980). In 1976 there were 1.7 million full-time and 2.2 million part-time students enrolled in community colleges; by 1986 there will be 2.1 million attending full time and 3.8 million attending part time ("20-Year Trends . . . ," 1978). In California, as early as 1972, part-time students comprised two thirds of the student body of the state's junior colleges—with over half of them more than twenty-one years of age (Knoell, 1976).

A recent Brookings Institution study, however, is less sanguine about the number of new "new students" who will wind up in two-year colleges. They see the likelihood of a "saturation of demand," effective competition from noncollegiate sectors, and the unwillingness of local, state, or federal governments to subsidize the education of working adults (Breneman and Nelson, 1980; Maeroff, 1980).

Nonetheless, large numbers of students will continue to be available in the future; the question is—what can or will the two-year college do to attract them, and what kinds of programs and services will they offer? The numbers are there because the baby boom of the 1950s will become the "adult boom" of the 1980s. During this decade, the fastest growing population cohort will be the twenty-five- to forty-five-year-olds—up from 62 to 78 million. And although these individuals attended college at the traditional age in greater percentage than ever before in history (largely because of the expansion of two-year colleges), literally millions were passed by or opted to defer their higher education.

For example, if during the 1960s, 70 percent of the high school population earned diplomas, and 60 percent of these graduates went on to college, and 50 percent of them received baccalaureates (all optimistic numbers), that leaves 72 percent of that 1960's group with an incomplete higher education; and they are all candidates for the kinds of programs community colleges have available for adult students.

A New Mission?

These shifts in population, this market of potential students has perhaps irrevocably altered the character and mission of the two-year college in America. The concept of the *comprehensive* community college was hard won from the early fathers of the junior college movement who largely saw the mission to embody programs that paralleled the first two years of an undergraduate education (Zwerling, 1976). During the 1950s and '60s, the comprehensive mission came to mean a balance between transfer, vocational, and community service programs. What we see now, with the predominance of adult part-time students, is a shift to what some have called the *community education function* of the two-year college (Cohen and Lombardi, 1979).

Much of what goes on under this rubric might have formerly been considered to be noncollegiate in nature: noncredit courses, remedial programs, Adult Basic Education, group counseling. Much that continues to resemble what goes on at four-year colleges and universities is changing in character. The transfer function for part-time students has become a casuality as the rush to vocational programs has been accelerated. Knoell (1976, p. 22) sees the emergence of students with "idiosyncratic objectives" who are not even interested in programs of one, much less two, year's duration. These students step in and out of school, often enrolling in a course that they stop attending after a few weeks or months as they achieve their objectives.

Knoell contends that this behavior explodes the "myth" that the community college is a two-year collegiate institution for recent high school graduates who attend continuously, and full time, while seeking preparation for entry level jobs or transfer to baccalaureate programs. Evidence for this includes the facts that (1) only a small fraction of part-time students enrolled for credit actually transfer; (2) many discontinue their attendance with fine academic records—43 percent of nonpersisters in her study of California junior colleges had GPAs of B or better after one term; and (3) there is a marked discrepancy between what students state to be their educational objectives and the courses and programs in which they actually enroll (Knoell, 1976; Knoell and others, 1976).

A statement of current reality—in Knoell's words: "Continuing education for part-time, adult students has become the dominant function of the community colleges"—should not be confused with the mission of the two-year college. Mission should never involve drifting in the direction in which the wind is blowing. If one were to adopt the view that mission follows enrollment patterns, it might then be said that this represents more a capitulation to success than a vision of institutional purpose.

Do we in fact want our two-year colleges to become merely subcollegiate technical institutes or centers for continuing education? Indeed, is this what students desire? No doubt noncredit programming is growing faster than credit (American Association of Community and Junior Colleges, 1979) and it is also true that part-time students drop in and out more than full-time; but does this mean that the comprehensive mission should be scuttled? An alternative analysis of Knoell's data may be useful here.

The Adult Student

Adult students are at least as capable of defining their educational objectives as traditional students. To claim, as Knoell does, that their quickly dropping out of courses, stepping in and out of school, and leaving while in good academic standing indicates part-time students' idiosyncratic achievement of limited academic objectives is to mock adulthood itself. To so casually discount what part-time students state to be their objectives may in fact be more an indictment of the inadequate counseling and advisement services received than any lack of clarity or precision on the part of students. If part-time students are incapable of stating their learning objectives, how can they find just what they need in a school's catalogue or decide just how long to remain in a course in order to attain their "actual" goals? It could also be that these students are not satisfied with what they encounter at college and that their leaving is an expression of frustration or discontent, as it so often is with traditional students.

Something else that needs careful examination is the demographics of part-time learners. It is a commonplace to note that they are older than full-time students. It is less well known that those who primarily benefit from lifelong learning are whiter, wealthier, and better educated than those who do not. And the trend has been to widen the inequalities that exist. For example, in 1969, 7.5 percent of the participants in continuing education were black. By 1975 blacks constituted only 6 percent of the adult student body. In 1969, in constant dollars, 55 percent of part-time students had incomes of more than $10,000; by 1975 the proportion had grown to 71 percent (Fiske, 1977; Rosenthal, 1977). With financial aid formulas penalizing part-time students and tuition reimbursement plans available only to the employed, the growth in adult education has enlarged the gaps between black and white, rich and poor, the schooled and the unschooled.

If community colleges want to contribute to the narrowing of these gaps and remain "people's colleges" and if they wish to continue to try to provide open access and succeed in their mission to serve the comprehensive needs of students at all levels of skill, offering programs that can be reasonably expected to work, it is imperative that two-year colleges base their services and offerings on the needs and real aspirations of their new "new students." Among other things, this means that colleges stop treating adult part-time students as if they were traditional students with lighter course loads (Eddy, 1978).

To help in the process of developing effective programs for adults, it is wise to be aware of what has recently been learned about the motivation of part-time learners. Motivational typologies, for example, have been put forth: Morstain and Smart (1977) delineate five categories of adult learners—nondirectional, social, stimulation-seeker, career oriented, and life change. Studies have been conducted to determine what part-time learners themselves see to be their needs for programs and services. The Returning Adult Student Project, conducted at six community colleges in New York state, found marked differences between perceived needs of full- and part-time students. The former were primarily concerned with social and personal development; the latter with vocational and skills improvement and formats to accelerate learning—independent study, life experience credit, fewer class meetings per week (Mangano and Corrado, 1979).

All too often, however, the kinds of programs and services adults require do not exist. One national survey of the services two-year colleges provide for part-time students found that fewer than one institution in five offers any kind of orientation program, only one in two provides counseling, barely one in five has special financial aid programs, less than 5 percent have childcare services in the evening (though 25 percent offer these services during the day to full-time students). This study concludes: "The part-time student is a welcome customer, but one who is definitely not accorded much attention or service by the institution" (Kegel, 1977, p. 41).

Successful Programs

It is a rare institution, indeed, that offers an integrated array of offerings and support services for its growing population of adult learners. But there are enough examples of successful individual initiatives at two- and four-year colleges to draw together a model for what might better be done to serve this new clientele.

First, for degree-seeking students (and there are many more than Knoell would contend) colleges should consider developing special degree programs for adults. The best of these programs are found in four-year colleges such as the University of Oklahoma's Bachelor of Liberal Studies or Queens College's ACE Program. These special programs have many similar qualities: general education requirements are consolidated into a series of interdisciplinary seminar-like courses that combine in-class and independent study. In this way, adults can earn a maximum number of credits in a minimum amount of time at the school itself. This is felt to be a valid format as adults are generally able to learn well independently. Often the same group of twenty to thirty students move together, semester to semester, through the required core of seminars. A sense of community quickly develops, and as a result of the peer support that inevitably occurs, a much greater than usual percentage of participants remain in school and eventually earn degrees.

There are of course a growing number of noncampus learning opportunities available to adults. The External Degree Program in New York State, Chicago's City-Wide Institute, and Edison College in New Jersey are just three examples. In addition, there is a great deal of recent interest in so-called "remote learning" where students remain at home and receive lessons via cable television. It may be that technology is such that each home can become a learning center, an "electronic cottage" in Toffler's (1980) words, but there are hidden human costs here — there is enough alienation in modern life without compounding it by an excessive use of electronic media and solitary study.

Without doubt there is great need for entry or transition programs for adults that concentrate on sharpening rusty academic and study skills and the dissemination of current information on financial aid, admissions, registration procedures, and curricular offerings. In addition, effective transition programs offer the opportunity for returning students to discuss and deal with those personal, family, and work-related questions they routinely face when the pressures of school are added to their lives. At Clackamas Community College in Oregon, there is a Confidence Clinic that was designed to help women on welfare achieve and maintain self-sufficiency. It provides opportunities for self-evaluation, vocational and personality testing, and personal problem solving (Weiss, 1978). At the City University of New York, four colleges developed a Preadmission Counseling Program to encourage women to explore their educational and vocational potential (Chitayat and Hymer, 1976). At Michigan's Schoolcraft Community College, a Human Potential Seminar was established to help adult students overcome anxieties about returning to college (Burnside, 1974). New York University's School of Continuing Education, Adult Transition Program offers a wide array of courses, workshops, and individual advisement designed for adults who want to gain the confidence and skills they need to return to school and do well when enrolled, change careers, or find new direction for their lives (*New York University* . . . , 1980).

Many colleges have opted not to offer support services to their part-time students. Obviously cost is a major factor. More troublesome is the notion that adults require fewer services than traditional students—after all, to be adult means having the skills and self-knowledge needed to negotiate the world, including school. Actually, adults often need more services than full-time students who have moved through school without interruptions and thus know the ropes and have more academic confidence. In addition, one frequently encounters a closed system in which the college staff assumes their adult students are adapting effectively and succeeding academically (as they hear nothing to the contrary) while these students, who are floundering academically and questioning the meaning and validity of having returned to college, suffer in silence. Their inner dialogue often assumes that as adults they should be able to still their self-doubts and succeed without special assistance. Too often, in the absence of well-conceived support services, part-time student drift away in seeming self-defeat.

Dangers of Lifelong Learning

There are drawbacks in lifelong learning as well. One must strike that delicate balance between support and challenge. If some colleges have been remiss in providing services, others have begun to see the community education function as synonymous with the establishment of therapeutic communities for students. Rockland Community College (New York), for example, offers a weekend Family College where parents and children attend together. More than courses are available and more than additional income for the institution is the issue. In the dean's words: "As enrollments decline, community colleges are taking a harder look at the service commitment. It isn't enough for education to prepare people for the world of work — we must *maintain* them through their lifetime" (italics added; Katz, 1978, p. 38). The potential tyranny of lifelong learning appears. In Rockland's course in kite flying, the activity is secondary — "the main purpose is to earmark those two Saturday hours for the family" (p. 39). In spite of the temptation to have school-based lifelong learning finally and fully replace family and church as sources for upbringing, socialization, and education, the community college must define a more secure and appropriate mission for itself.

"New" new students have been important to community colleges for several years. Their numbers will increase in the 1980's and schools must give them intelligent consideration. During recent years, under intensive budgetary pressure, new "new students" have been attractive mainly because of their FTE power. This power is both awesome and important to the future of two-year colleges. Too often, these students' academic potential is unrealized as the majority fail to complete their educational plans. In part this "failure" is the result of institutional greed: collect the tuition, fees, state subsidies; offer classes taught almost exclusively by part-time faculty; provide little or no advisement and counseling; and during evening hours shut down even the cafeteria and bookstore. This is a short-sighted approach — even in bottom line terms. Recruitment and enrollment is only one side of the FTE story; retention (the result of students having successful experiences) is the other. And, as has been seen, there are many models to draw upon to provide these opportunities.

References

American Association of Community and Junior Colleges. *1979 Community, Junior, and Technical College Directory.* Ed. F. Gilbert. Washington: American Association of Community and Junior Colleges, 1979.

Breneman, D. W., and Nelson, S. C. *Setting National Priorities: Agenda for the 1980's.* Washington: Brookings Institution, 1980.

Burnside, R. W. "Group Counseling Techniques for Adults Returning to College." *Journal of College Student Personnel,* January 1974, *15* (1), 62.

Chitayat, D., and Hymer, S. *The New Occupational Student: The Mature Adult Woman. A Preadmission Counseling Program in Four CUNY Community Colleges.* Albany: City University of New York, New York Institute for Research and Development in Occupational Education; New York State Education Dept., Office of Occupational and Continuing Education, August, 1976. 129pp. (ED 138 877).

Cohen, A. M., and Lombardi, J. "Can the Community College Survive Success?" *Change,* 1979, *11* (8), 24–27.

Eddy, M. S. "Part-Time Students." *Research Currents.* Washington: American Association for Higher Education; ERIC Clearinghouse on Higher Education, June 1978.

Fiske, E. B. "Programs for Adults Bypass Neediest." *New York Times,* September 10, 1977, pp. 1, 11.

Katz, M. "All in the Family." *Change,* 1978, 10 (5), 38–39.

Kegel, P. L. "Community and Junior College Concern for and Services Provided to Part-Time Students." March 1977. 62pp. (ED 138 324).

Knoell, D. "Challenging the 'Model and the Myth'." *Community and Junior College Journal,* 1976, *47* (3), 22–25.

Knoell, D., and others. "Through the Open Door: A Study of Patterns of Enrollment and Performance in California's Community Colleges." Sacramento: California State Postsecondary Commission, February 1976. 82pp. (ED 119 752).

Maeroff, G. I. "Colleges, Pressed for Students, Grow Less Selective." *New York Times,* April 4, 1980, pp. 1, A12.

Mangano, J. A., and Corrado, T. J. *Meeting Academic Success Needs of Re-entry Adults. Final Report.* Albany: State University of New York, Two Year College Student Development Center, 1979. 47pp. (ED 169 967).

Morstain, B. R., and Smart, J. C. "A Motivational Typology of Adult Learners." *Journal of Higher Education,* 1977, *48* (6), 665–679.

New York University School of Continuing Education Bulletin. Spring 1980. New York: New York University Press, 1980.

Rosenthal, E. L. "Lifelong Learning—For Some of the People." *Change,* 1977, *9* (8), 44–45.

Scully, M. G. "Volatile Decade Predicted for Community Colleges." *Chronicle of Higher Education,* March 31, 1980, p. 6.

Toffler, A. *The Third Wave.* New York: Morrow, 1980.

"20-Year Trends in Higher Education: Fact File." *Chronicle of Higher Education,* November 13, 1978, p. 13. Source: National Center for Education Statistics.

Weiss, M. "The Confidence Clinic: A Program in Self-Esteem, Independence, and Career Planning." Oregon City, Oregon: Clackamas Community College. November 1978. 7pp. (ED 161 476).

Zwerling, L. S. *Second Best: The Crisis of the Community College.* New York: McGraw-Hill, 1976.

L. Steven Zwerling is associate dean of continuing education at New York University

*Further resources from the ERIC Clearinghouse for
Junior Colleges can provide opinions on the mission
of the community colleges in the 1980s.*

Sources and Information: Questioning the Community College Role

Donna Dzierlenga
Donna Sillman

This concluding chapter provides additional citations from ERIC documents relating to issues the community colleges will face in the years ahead. The references include both general discussions of the community colleges' future and more specific examinations of the various roles they will play. Unfortunately, lack of space prohibits lengthy description of these resources.

The ERIC documents (ED numbers) listed, unless otherwise indicated, are available on microfiche (MF) or in paper copy (PC) from the ERIC Document Reproduction Service (EDRS), Computer Microfilm International Corporation, P. O. Box 190, Arlington, VA 22210. The MF price for documents under 480 pages is $0.83. Prices for PC are: 1–25 pages, $1.82; 26–50 pages, $3.32; 51–75 pages, $4.82; 76–100 pages, $6.32. For materials having more than 100 pages, add $1.50 for each 25-page increment (or fraction thereof). Postage must be added to all orders. Abstracts of these and other documents in the junior college collection are available upon request from the ERIC Clearinghouse for Junior Colleges, 96 Powell Library, University of California, Los Angeles, CA 90024. Bracketed publication dates are approximate.

Future of the Community College

Angel, D., and Sharp, S. *Commission on the Future: Final Recommendations.* Imperial, Calif.: Imperial Valley College, 1979. 33pp. (ED 175 488 — Available in microfiche only.)

Callan, P. M. *California Post-Secondary Education: Challenges and Constraints in California Higher Education.* Hayward, Calif.: Chabot College, 1979. 8pp. (ED 181 970)

Cosand, J. P. *Perspective: Community Colleges in the 1980s. Horizon Issues Monograph Series.* Washington, D.C.: American Association of Community and Junior Colleges, Council of Universities and Colleges; and Los Angeles: ERIC Clearinghouse for Junior Colleges, 1979. 63pp. (ED 178 146)

Marsee, S. E. *Patterns Influencing Community College Change.* Unpublished paper, 1978. 14pp. (ED 156 269)

Marty, M. A. (Ed.). *New Directions for Community Colleges: Responding to New Missions,* no. 24. San Francisco: Jossey-Bass, 1978. (Available from Jossey-Bass, Inc., 433 California Street, San Francisco, Calif. 94104, $6.95.

Proceedings [of the] Annual Governor's Workshop for Community College Trustees (1st, Tallahassee, Florida, August 5–6, 1977). Tallahassee: Florida State Department of Education, Division of Community Colleges, 1977. 41pp. (ED 151 060)

Tillery, D. *Meritocracy II. Perspectives on the Church and the Community College, Paper Number Sixteen.* Portland, Ore.: United Ministries in Higher Education, [1979]. 18pp. (ED 176 828)

Tschechtelin, J. D. *Looking Back on Community Colleges in the 1980's: A Stimulus Paper. "August, 1989."* Unpublished paper, 1979. 9pp. (ED 178 130)

Weiner, S. S. *Teaching and the Collegiate Idea.* Speech presented before the Academic Senate of the California Community Colleges, Sacramento, Calif., April 6, 1978. 12pp. (ED 153 672)

Young, D., and others. *Critical Issues for Tennessee Community Colleges. College of Education Monograph Series, No. 10.* Knoxville: University of Tennessee, Bureau of Educational Research and Service, 1978. 89pp. (ED 178 147)

General Education

Cohen, A. M. *The Case for General Education in Community Colleges.* Paper presented at the Forum on Future Purposes, Content, and Formats for the General Education of Community College Students, Montgomery College, Md., May 22, 1978. 43pp. (ED 154 849)

Preusser, J. W. *General Education: Refrain or Retain.* Unpublished paper, 1978. 12pp. (ED 168 632)

Sanborn, D. H. *Why All CCC Students Need General Education: A Position Paper in Support of Resolutions Proposed by the City Colleges Study Group.* Paper prepared for the "Education: Planning for the Quality 80s" conference, Chicago, Ill., November 30–December 1, 1979. 21pp. (ED 180 519)

Vocational Education

The Academic Crossover Report. Community Colleges, Fall 1978. Honolulu: University of Hawaii, Community College System, 1978. 17pp. (ED 165 819—Available in microfiche only.)

Clowes, D., and Levin, B. *The Cooling Out Function Reconsidered.* Unpublished paper, [1978]. 15pp. (ED 172 899)

Ferguson, R. T. *A Study of Open Entry–Open Exit Programs in Vocational Education. Institutional Research Report No. 78/79-6.* Perkinson, Miss.: Mississippi Gulf Coast Junior College, 1979. 15 pp. (ED 169 998)

Korin, A. S. *Education and Work in the Future.* Paper presented at the Conference on the Future of Work and the Community College, Texas City, Tex., October 19, 1978. 27pp. (ED 161 504)

Lateral and Vertical Student Mobility: An Essential for the Community College. Atlanta: Southern Regional Education Board, 1977. 23pp. (ED 148 421)

Lombardi, J. *Resurgence of Occupational Education. Topical Paper Number 65.* Los Angeles: ERIC Clearinghouse for Junior Colleges, 1978. 41pp. (ED 148 418)

Pincus, F. L. *Tracking and Vocational Education in Community Colleges.* Paper presented at the Convention of the Society for the Study of Social Problems, San Francisco, Calif., 1978. 55pp. (ED 175 504)

Transfer Education

California Community College Students Who Transfer. A Continuation of Through the Open Door. A Study of Patterns of Enrollment and Performance in California's Community Colleges. Sacramento: California State Postsecondary Education Commission, 1979. 50pp. (ED 171 350)

Lombardi, J. *The Decline of Transfer Education. Topical Paper Number 70.* Los Angeles: ERIC Clearinghouse for Junior Colleges, 1979. 37pp. (ED 179 273)

Rooth, S. R. *The Reverse Transfer Student at Northampton County Area Community College.* Unpublished paper, 1979. 53pp. (ED 178 122)

Stevenson, J. A. *Materially Disadvantaged Students and the Transfer Function of Community College.* Unpublished paper, 1979. 7pp. (ED 172 882)

Community Education and Services

Gianini, P. C., Jr. *Community-Based Educaion: A Team Approach.* Paper presented at the American Association of Community and Junior

Colleges Conference, Malta, Ill., October 19, 1979. 14pp. (ED 178 134)

Harlacher, E. L., and Gollattscheck, J. F. (Eds.). *New Directions for Community Colleges: Implementing Community-Based Education*, no. 21. San Francisco: Jossey-Bass, 1978. (Available from Jossey-Bass, Inc., Publishers, 433 California Street, San Francisco, Calif. 94104, $6.95)

Lombardi, J. *Community Education: Threat to College Status? Topical Paper No. 68.* Los Angeles: ERIC Clearinghouse for Junior Colleges, 1978. 45pp. (ED 156 296)

Young, R. B., and others. *Directions for the Future: An Analysis of the Community Services Dimension of Community Colleges. Community Colleges, Community Education Monograph #2.* Washington, D.C.: American Association of Community and Junior Colleges, National Center for Community Education; Ann Arbor: University of Michigan, Office of Community Education Research, 1978. 70pp. (ED 158 787)

Education for Adult, Nontraditional, and Underprepared Students

Charles, R. F., and Perkins, M. *The Development of an Alernative to Proposition 13 Losses in Student Services for Non-Traditional Students. The DIAL Program for Students at the Sunnyvale Center.* Cupertino, Calif.: De Anza College, 1978. 14pp. (ED 160 142)

Creamer, D. G., and Clowes, D. A. *Student Development: Mainstream or Penumbra?* Unpublished paper, [1978]. 28pp. (ED 168 636)

Fuller, J. W. *Continuing Education and the Community College.* Chicago: Nelson-Hall, 1979. 112pp. (Available from Nelson-Hall, Inc., Publishers, 111 North Canal Street, Chicago, Ill. 60606, $12.95)

Gollattscheck, J. F. *Institutional Commitment to Funding Adult Learning Programs.* Speech given before the National Council on Community Services and Continuing Education Conference, Miami, Fla., May 17–19, 1978. 15pp. (ED 156 253)

Herd, R. H. *Developmental Studies: Whose Responsibility?* Paper presented at the National Conference on Innovations, Diffusion, and Delivery in Education, Newport Beach, Calif., March 6–8, 1978. 12pp. (ED 156 223)

Jones, A. P., Jr. *Providing for the Underprepared College Student.* Unpublished paper, [1979]. 9pp. (ED 181 945)

White, R. A. *The Effectiveness of Bottom-Line Services for Today's Student: A Study of Nine Colleges.* Unpublished paper, 1978. 41pp. (ED 157 566)

Lifelong Learning/Reverse Transfers

Grafton, C. L., and Roy, D. D. *The "Second-Time Around" Community College Students: Assessment of Reverse Transfer Student Performance in a*

University Setting. Paper presented at the annual meeting of the American Educational Research Association, Boston, Mass., April 7–11, 1980. 33p. (ED 184 620)

Heermann, B., Enders, C. C., and Wine, E. (Eds.). *New Directions for Community Colleges: Serving Lifelong Learners,* no. 29. San Francisco: Jossey-Bass, 1980. (Available from Jossey-Bass Inc., Publishers, 433 California Street, San Francisco, Calif. 94104, $6.95)

Peters, J. K. *Lifelong Learners: The Community College Adult Student with a Bachelor's Or Higher Degree.* Unpublished paper, 1978. 26pp. (ED 153 666 — Available in microfiche only.)

Wilcox, P. *Counseling for Second Careers.* Unpublished paper, 1978. 19pp. (ED 160 174)

Minority Education

Beckwith, M. M., and Edwards, S. J. *Ethnic Minorities in Two-Year Colleges: Report to the Higher Education Research Institute.* Los Angeles: Center for the Study of Community Colleges, 1979. 107pp. (ED 176 831)

Brawer, F. B. *Trends in Ethnic Enrollments. Junior College Resource Review.* Los Angeles: ERIC Clearinghouse for Junior Colleges, 1979. 6pp. (ED 164 056)

Cohen, A. M. *The Minority Student Controversy. Junior College Resource Review.* Los Angeles: ERIC Clearinghouse for Junior Colleges, 1980. 6pp. (ED 183 228)

de los Santos, A. G., Jr. *Hispanics in the Community/Junior Colleges: Donde Estamos en el Ano 1978.* Paper presented at the National Conference on the Education of Hispanics, Washington, D.C., August 20–23, 1978. 37pp. (ED 180 509)

Tschechtelin, J. D. *Black and White Students in Maryland Community Colleges.* Annapolis: Maryland State Board for Community Colleges, 1979. 20pp. (ED 175 513)

Student Objectives

Brunner, W. D., and others. *Retention and Attrition: Does It Relate to Students' Goals?* Paper presented at the annual meeting of the American Education Research Association, Toronto, Canada, March 27, 1978. 15pp. (ED 153 682)

Mason, S. E. *Goal Dissonance in the Community College: A Case Study.* Paper presented at the annual meeting of the American Educational Research Association, Toronto, Canada, March 27–31, 1978. 22pp. (ED 152 377)

Validation Study on the Classification of Non-Curricular Students, Fall 1976. Richmond: Virginia State Department of Community Colleges, 1979. 17pp. (ED 153 683)

Financing

Augenblick, J. *Issues in Financing Community Colleges.* Denver, Colo.: Education Commission of the States, Education Finance Center, 1978. 70pp. (ED 164 020)

Bers, J. A. *Tying Resources to Results: Integrating the Resource Allocation Process into Planning and Management in a Public Two-Year College.* Paper presented to the American Educational Research Association Special Interest Group for Community Colleges, Williamsburg, Va., July 18–19, 1978. 50pp. (ED 164 021)

Financial Support for Community Colleges: A Bibliographic Summary with Abstracts. Phoenix, Ariz.: Maricopa County Community College District, 1979. 32pp. (ED 168 645)

Martorana, S. V., and Wattenbarger, J. L. *Principles, Practices, and Alternatives in State Methods of Financing Community Colleges and an Approach to Their Evaluation, with Pennsylvania a Case State. Report No. 32.* University Park: Pennsylvania State University, Center for the Study of Higher Education, 1978. 65pp. (ED 158 807)

Donna Dzierlenga is User Services Specialist at the ERIC Clearinghouse for Junior Colleges.

Donna Sillman is bibliographer at the ERIC Clearinghouse for Junior Colleges.

Index

STATEMENT OF OWNERSHIP, MANAGEMENT, AND CIRCULATION
(Required by 39 U.S.C. 3685)

1. Title of Publication: New Directions for Community Colleges. A. Publication number: USPS 121-710. 2. Date of filing: September 29, 1980. 3. Frequency of issue: quarterly. A. Number of issues published annually: four. B. Annual subscription price: $30 institutions; $18 individuals. 4. Location of known office of publication: 433 California Street, San Francisco (San Francisco County), California 94104. 5. Location of the headquarters or general business offices of the publishers: 433 California Street, San Francisco (San Francisco County), California 94104. 6. Names and addresses of publisher, editor, and managing editor: publisher—Jossey-Bass Inc., Publishers, 433 California Street, San Francisco, California 94104; editor—Arthur Cohen, ERIC, 96 Powell Library Bldg., U.C.L.A., Los Angeles, CA 90024; managing editor—JB Lon Hefferlin, 433 California Street, San Francisco, California 94104. 7. Owner: Jossey-Bass Inc., Publishers, 433 California Street, San Francisco, California 94104. 8. Known bondholders, mortgages, and other security holders owning or holding 1 percent or more of total amount of bonds, mortgages, or other securities: same as No. 7. 10. Extent and nature of circulation: (Note: first number indicates the average number of copies of each issue during the preceding twelve months; the second number indicates the actual number of copies published nearest to filing date.) A. Total number of copies printed (net press run): 2503, 2540. B. Paid circulation, 1) Sales through dealers and carriers, street vendors, and counter sales: 85, 40. 2) Mail subscriptions: 1076, 949. C. Total paid circulation: 1161, 989. D. Free distribution by mail, carrier, or other means (samples, complimentary, and other free copies): 275, 275. E. Total distribution (sum of C and D): 1436, 1264. F. Copies not distributed, 1) Office use, left over, unaccounted, spoiled after printing: 1067, 1276. 2) Returns from news agents: 0, 0. G. Total (sum of E, F1, and 2 — should equal net press run shown in A): 2503, 2540.

I certify that the statements made by me above are correct and complete.

JOHN R. WARD
Vice-President